Designing with Tile

Designing with Tile

Carolyn Coyle

VAN NOSTRAND REINHOLD
I(T)P A Division of International Thomson Publishing, Inc.

New York • Albany • Bonn • Boston • Detroit • London • Madrid • Melbourne
Mexico City • Paris • San Francisco • Singapore • Tokyo • Toronto

To my family, friends, and fellow tile enthusiasts who made this book possible.

Copyright © 1995 by Carolyn Coyle
Designed by Carolyn Coyle

Published by Van Nostrand Reinhold

I(T)P™ A division of International Thomson Publishing, Inc.
The ITP logo is a trademark under license

Printed in Hong Kong

For more information, contact:

Van Nostrand Reinhold
115 Fifth Avenue
New York, NY 10003

International Thomson Publishing GmbH
Königswinterer Strasse 418
53227 Bonn
Germany

International Thomson Publishing Europe
Berkshire House 168-173
High Holborn
London WCIV 7AA
England

International Thomson Publishing Asia
221 Henderson Road #05-10
Henderson Building
Singapore 0315

Thomas Nelson Australia
102 Dodds Street
South Melbourne, 3205
Victoria, Australia

International Thomson Publishing Japan
Hirakawacho Kyowa Building, 3F
2-2-1 Hirakawacho
Chiyoda-ku, 102 Tokyo
Japan

Nelson Canada
1120 Birchmount Road
Scarborough, Ontario
Canada M1K 5G4

International Thomson Editores
Campos Eliseos 385, Piso 7
Col. Polanco
11560 Mexico D.F. Mexico

2 3 4 5 6 7 8 9 10 CP 01 00 99 98 97 96 95

Library of Congress Cataloging-in-Publication Data

Coyle, Carolyn.
Designing with Tile / Carolyn Coyle.
p.   cm.
Includes bibliographical references and index.
ISBN 0-442-01731-6
1. Tiles in interior decoration. 2. Tiles—Design. I. Title.
NK2115.5.T54C68 1995   94-15136
747'.9—dc20   CIP

Contents

Acknowledgments

*T*his book simply would not have been possible without the support of fellow tile enthusiasts in the United States, Europe, and beyond. These enthusiasts came in many different forms: as architects, designers, and tile manufacturers, large and small, as well as tile artists, contractors, and consultants to the ceramic tile industry. Most of the photography contained in the book was supplied by these tile enthusiasts, and to each one I am indebted.

More specifically, I wish to thank Peter Johnson, Jr., Chairman of the Tile Promotion Board, for his assistance with the project and for reviewing several chapters. Also thanks to Joe Taylor and the Tile Heritage Foundation for publicizing the project, and to Robert Kleinhans and Ken Erikson at the Tile Council of America for technical assistance and permission to reproduce excerpts from the TCA handbook. Additional thanks to Joe Tarver and the National Tile Contractors Association for use of the NTCA glossary and to Dan O'Brien and Harrop Industries for his input on the section on manufacturing. The Italian Tile Center and the Gura Agency were also most helpful, offering more than 100 photographs for my use. The Ceramic Tile Distributors Association also offered their extensive library of photography. Michael Byrne, Robert Young, and Jess McIlvain, all experts in the field of ceramic tile, also provided valuable information and a critique of the technical chapters.

Additional thanks are due to my family, friends, and colleagues who contributed in one way or another. In their own way, each provided encouragement, criticism and assistance. Thanks to Jody van den Heuvel for the painstaking task of editing much of the manuscript and to Chrissy Mizak for

the drawings on pages 156 and 157. Also thanks to Ellen Yossarian, Harvey Powell, Bret Parsons, Rita St. Clair, Scott Sider, Caren Forsten, Sally Sessions, Donald Meserlian, Win Boyer, and Jeremy Kilborn for assistance with the text and photography selection. The support of Debbie Shirley, Louise Lay, Lisa Meyer, Jason Bober, Janet Shenk, Mary Coyle, Bob Soltysiak, Mike Knapp, Dave Miller, Kostas Damalas, Roger Miller, and W. C. are also greatly appreciated.

Lastly, special thanks to Wendy Lochner, Mike Suh, Jane Degenhardt, Anthony Calcara, and Van Nostrand Reinhold for believing in the concept. Writing this book was, as it should be, the experience of a lifetime.

C. C.
Baltimore, Maryland

Foreword

Who would think that by combining dirt, fire, and water one could create a beautiful, functional construction material? Ever since human beings first combined these materials various people have strived to modify and improve this product—from the first cave dwellers who realized that you can form clay for pottery, bricks, and tiles to present-day tile manufacturers.

This evolution of ceramic tile has resulted in an incredible selection of millions of different colors, shapes, sizes, and textures. The ability to create something new or to reinvent something old is infinite. What was once only available to nobility, churches, and the wealthy is now affordable by all people.

Carolyn Coyle's fine book will help you understand this evolution, inspire you with the beauty and diversity of tile, and assist you in your selection process. As with anything else, if ceramic tiles are used in the wrong way, the results can be disappointing. By acquainting yourself with some basics you will be able to make an informed decision when you select ceramic tile for your home or project. A properly selected and installed room with ceramic tile can last forever, if so desired, or can be replaced periodically as design trends change.

The inherent beauty, ease of maintenance, affordability, energy efficiency, and hygienically safe characteristics of ceramic tile make it the surface of the future.

Peter Johnson, Jr.
Chairman, Tile Promotion Board

Designing with Tile

Chapter 1

Understanding Tiles

*F*ew finish materials can match the impact of ceramic tiles on architecture and interior design. As one of the most enduring building materials, ceramic tile is inherently beautiful, versatile, functional, and permanent.

Ceramic tile has been in use for thousands of years, and though manufacturing processes have changed considerably, it is still essentially just cut pieces of fired clay. Through manipulation of size, shape, color, and texture, these pieces of clay offer the full range of decorative possibilities. A small kitchen takes on a rustic simplicity with a blue and white delft tile backsplash and an earthy red quarry tile floor. In contrast, a private bath exhibits an understated elegance with monochromatic polished paver tiles cladding both walls and floors. From the provincial to the most sleek and sophisticated designs, ceramic tile can create any atmosphere you desire.

Undeniably, ceramic tile is one of the most functional finish materials created by man. It resists water, staining, and heat and is exceptionally durable and easy to maintain. Because of these qualities, ceramic tile is well suited for a variety of uses, including floors, walls, ceilings, countertops, fireplaces, stairs, and exterior applications. No other finish material can make such a claim for wide-ranging use. History proves ceramic tile's versatility and permanence, since it has been successfully used in ancient Roman pavements, medieval cathedrals, and Renaissance homes. In 20th-century America, ceramic tile still enjoys enormous popularity, adding beauty and value to both new and remodeled homes.

Because of the enormous popularity of tiles, they are now available in a seemingly endless variety. From brightly glazed wall tiles and decorative accents to mosaics and quarry tiles, there are more options available than even the most savvy consumer or specifier can fathom. According to the Tile Council of America (TCA), there are over 25 major tile factories in the United States alone. These factories produce a myriad of standard production colors, sizes, and types of tile. In addition, custom colors, patterns, and textures can be manufactured to meet the requirements of special conditions. Factors such as the composition of the clay body, type and hardness of glaze, firing temperatures, dimensions, surface finish, and abrasive additives can all be manipulated to create an array of tiles with varying characteristics.

Because of this enormous variety, it is important to have a basic understanding of tile in order to make an appropriate selection. Such an understanding includes knowing the different types of tile and their characteristics, as well as considering the service demands for each application. In the United States, the American National Standards Institute (ANSI) has defined several groups of ceramic tile and set standards for their manufacture. This standard is the American National Standard Specifications for Ceramic Tile, ANSI A137.1. It includes several test methods devised by the

American Society for Testing and Materials (ASTM). These tests are used to verify the physical characteristics of the various types of tile. It should be noted that ANSI A137.1 is a voluntary standard and manufacturers do not have to comply. Tiles that do comply with the standard meet high standards of quality and manufacturers are encouraged to indicate this in their advertising.

While it is important to understand the types of tile and their characteristics, one must also consider aesthetics and the decorative effect of tile. Just because a tile has the appropriate performance characteristics does not in itself mean that it is the right tile. Color, texture, size, and shape must also be considered to provide a look that will enhance the space in which it is to be placed. Both function and aesthetic must work in harmony for a tile selection to be appropriate. In later chapters we will review the wide range of choices and styles available.

In addition, I am increasingly convinced that ceramic tile is the best choice in finish materials for many applications. Though initial costs for tile are sometimes higher, its life cycle costs are lower than for most other finish materials, including carpet, vinyl, and wood. Tile doesn't stain like carpet, scratch and burn like vinyl, or warp and rot like wood.

History

The architect and philosopher Christopher Alexander wrote, "There is one timeless way of building. It is thousands of years old, and the same today as it has always been." Certainly, ceramic tile is the essence of timeless design. Its enduring beauty and functionality appealed equally to Egyptian pharaohs, the 17th-century Dutch middle class, and modern America. From the ancient Mesopotamian ziggurats to the United States Capitol, tile is a part of the rich history of the human race.

Trace the history of tile and you trace the history of mankind. Archaeologists sift through the earth in search of bits of broken ceramic, since it is one of the few materials that survives. Architectural historians study the architecture of the ancient Egyptians and examine the blue tile veneer of the Step Pyramid of Zoser at Sakhara. Antique delftware displays the scenes of 17th-century everyday life, in which children play and minstrels sing. Wars are fought and kingdoms conquered, and artisans pass on their unique knowledge of tilemaking to new cultures. Undeniably, our very understanding of ourselves is inextricably tied to these cut pieces of fired clay.

As the most abundant building material on earth, clay was first pressed into pottery and tiles by ancient civilization over 6000 years ago. Forming

▲ 1 Handmade ceramic tile sheathes these historic bridges in the Plaza de España in Sevilla, Spain.

techniques were simple, as the soft clay lent itself to digging and molding when damp. Though raw materials were abundant, tiles were not commonly available to the general public until the 16th century. What was once the exclusive right of royalty and the ecclesiastic became the decoration of choice for Dutch, English, and Spanish middle-class homes. An old Spanish proverb testifies to this fact, since "Only a poor man lives in a house without tiles."

Tile Through the Ages

Ancient Times

The art of making ceramic tile is as old as civilization itself. Only the manufacture of simple mud bricks predates the invention of ceramic tile. Tiles were first used in Neolithic times to protect their soft, sun-dried brick structures, but tiles soon became the means for ornamentation and beautification of temples and palaces. The great mud-brick ziggurats of Mesopotamia and the temples and palaces of Egypt and Babylon are examples of this method of construction, used throughout the first, second, and third millennium B.C. Glazed ceramic tile veneers of brilliant blue, brown, yellow, red, and black served to both protect and adorn these magnificent structures. Sometimes tiles were molded in bas-relief, incorporating designs of animals, birds, or high priests and repetitive, stylized patterns and borders. Indelibly recorded in these durable clay tiles are the intellectual achievements, battle triumphs, and religious beliefs of these ancient peoples.

Other early developments in ceramic tile include high-fired white tiles from China. These tiles are notable since they were the forerunners of Chinese porcelain. The first known use of glazed mosaic murals and pavements was by the Persians in the 6th century B.C. Persian techniques were then adopted by the Saracens and later by the Moors until the techniques reached their height in the 12th to 15th centuries in such structures as the Alhambra in Granada, Spain. Many of these ancient Persian ceramic techniques were later used in the production of tile throughout Europe.

The Medieval Period

Interest in decorative tiles began to flourish in the 12th to 16th centuries with the invention of encaustic tiles. These beautiful yet durable inlaid tiles were common in medieval Europe, particularly in England. They were first used in the 12th century as flooring in European cathedrals, as in Westminster Abbey, dating from 1255. Later in the century, some homes began to make use of these muted brown, blue, and gold patterned tiles. Individually handmade, the tiles display Eastern influences in their use of highly intricate, colored designs. Shallow relief designs were carved into the body of the tile and the resulting depressions were filled with contrasting colored clays. Another medieval tile, sgraffito, made use of a less common technique, where a thin layer of clay was scraped away, exposing a contrasting background. Tring Church in Hertfordshire, England, exhibits samples of 14th-century sgraffito tiles depicting the life of Christ.

Unfortunately, the English art of encaustic tilemaking was lost for several hundred years. This occurred because encaustic tiles were manufactured by monks whose monasteries were destroyed by Henry VIII in his break with the Roman Catholic church. For the next 300 years, all English tilemaking ceased, and new types of painted ceramic tiles were imported from Italy and Spain.

The Renaissance

Decorative tile continued to increase in popularity in the Renaissance as new techniques were created and ancient ones were revived. Painted decorative tiles were first produced in Spain, using the ancient Moorish technique of tin-lead glazes. By the 15th century, this technique had been transmitted to Italy, where it was called majolica. Both floor and wall tiles were made using this method of displaying elaborate multicolor designs. In the 16th and 17th centuries, Italian Renaissance ceramic painters were world renowned for the quality of their art. Using the majolica technique, they majestically presented the predominant themes of the Renaissance—mythology, illusion, and classical symbols. At the same time, a new ceramic technique was developed producing a flawless transparent glaze. The modern ceramic term, faience, is derived from these beautiful tiles that were first produced in 16th century Faenza, Italy.

As the spirit of the Renaissance spread through Europe, so did the techniques of tilemaking. In the Dutch city of Delft, blue figures depicting themes of everyday life were painted on a white tin glaze. Though the technique was not innovative, these tiles won wide acclaim for their quaintness and humor. Fireplaces, stove facings, bedrooms, signage, staircases, and cellars were favorite locations for these tiles, and the increase in trade resulted in many exports to England and later to America. By the 18th century, Dutch tilemaking was almost dead, but the craft lived on in England where the ceramic tile industry was reestablished. Soon after, England dominated the tile industry in both production output and the development of advanced techniques.

Modern Developments

In the 20th century, mass production techniques continued to improve, making tile more durable and accessible to consumers. The forerunners of modern manufacturing methods were developed in 18th and 19th century England. Pioneering English tilemakers soon brought these techniques to America. In the 1870s, both dust-pressed clay tile and encaustic tile were

▲ 2 Floor of the U.S. Capitol Building tiled in 1859 using English encaustic tile.

manufactured in the United States for the first time. By the 1880s, the popularity of tile rose to record proportions, and tile clubs met to hand-paint decorative tiles. Though ceramic tile is no longer a society fad, it continues to serve many important uses in both residential and commercial construction. Using both time-tested and new techniques, the modern ceramic tile industry provides an enormously varied selection of floor and wall tiles that are both durable and easy to clean.

Industrial ceramic companies are providing new applications for fired products that have reached beyond traditional uses to new space age technologies. The space shuttle, bioceramic implants, and nuclear power plants have all harnessed the strength of modern ceramic products. The durability and heat resistance of ceramics is stretched to new limits as completely new classes of materials are developed for these applications. As one of the first handcrafted utilitarian products, ceramic items continue to improve our lives by meeting the needs of our modern industrial society.

▲ 3 Four-tile encaustic panel manufactured in England.

Advancements in Manufacturing

Since the early part of the 20th century, most ceramic tiles are mass-produced in automated manufacturing facilities. Handmade tile, once the staple of the industry, has become a comparative rarity. In the United States alone, sophisticated computerized equipment efficiently produces more than 500 million square feet per year. Some of the larger facilities are able to turn out more than 150,000 square feet per day.

Modern manufacturing has developed several processes for forming ceramic tiles, of which two are the most commonly employed: dust-press and extrusion. Both of these methods produce tile with unique characteristics and a distinctive appearance.

Dust-press tiles are appropriately named because the tile body has been dried to almost a dust consistency before it is pressed into shape. The process begins when raw materials, usually including talc and natural clays, are pulverized, mixed with water, and dried. Large hydraulic presses force this dustlike clay into dies to create the desired shape. Depending on the manufacturing process, the tile can be single or double fired. Most wall tiles and trim shapes are dust-pressed. They are characteristically uniform in appearance with minimal warpage, wedging, and variation in thickness.

The extruded process mixes raw materials such as clay, shale, and water to form a plastic mud. An extruder forces this material through a die, and while still plastic, cuts it to the desired size for firing. All quarry tile and some mosaics are manufactured by this method. Because they are extruded, these tiles show variations in size and thickness. Some manufacturers grind these tiles after firing to eliminate the variations and create a more uniform appearance.

Unfired, formed clay, known as green tiles, become ceramic tiles with the application of heat. Many automated factories use roller hearth kilns in which the green tiles are moved along metal or ceramic rollers through a series of chambers in the kiln. This is the most fuel-efficient method of firing tiles. Firing temperatures in these kilns are typically around 2000° F. The precise firing temperature and amount of time in the kiln are two important factors that affect the degree of vitrification, absorption level, precise size, and appearance of the tile.

As previously mentioned, green tiles can be either single- or double-fired. Many glazed wall tiles are produced using the single fire process in conventional tunnel kilns. Other glazed wall tiles are double fired since this method allows for the creation of high-gloss glazes. First, the green tiles are fired to create a bisque, then the bisque is glazed and refired. In contrast, most glazed and unglazed floor tiles are single fired in roller hearth kilns.

Glaze formulas for both single- and double-fired tiles are the property of the manufacturer. Because the residual manufacturing waste is safer for the environment, more and more tile companies are developing lead-free glazes.

Quality control inspections occur throughout the manufacturing process for all types of tile. Upon completion, the finished products are graded as either standards, seconds, or culls depending on surface blemishes, warpage, color, size, and general appearance. These characteristics are usually evaluated in accordance with the standards set out in ANSI A137.1. In packaging, standards and seconds are clearly marked and sold as such. Culls are usually crushed for other uses.

Automated Factory Tour: TileCera

Perhaps the best way to understand the design and manufacture of ceramic tile is to tour a modern automated factory, where these products are being developed and mass-produced. A new manufacturing plant built for TileCera in Clarksville, Tennessee, shows the level of sophistication modern manufacturers are bringing to the production of ceramic tiles.

TileCera, which manufacturers the Esquire line of floor and wall tiles, is the first manufacturing company established by Thailand on American soil. TileCera is a joint venture between the Siam Cement Corporation and Finfloor, a leading Italian tile producer.

Arriving at the plant, the first thing you notice is its size: 337,500 square feet, more than eight acres under one roof. The facility's long narrow

◄ 4 A uniquely designed multi-chamber concrete silo stores and protects raw materials while reducing airborne dust.

shape has a practical purpose: tiles are moved in a smooth, almost continual flow through the various stages of body preparation, pressing, glazing, and firing. The structure is designed for easy expansion along one side as production increases, with complete new lines simply placed beside existing equipment.

The plant's concern for environmental issues is also evident. Designed to be among the most environmentally sensitive plants of its kind, the facility is dominated at one end by a storage silo that rises 150 feet into the air. Formed of concrete to a special design, the silo features multiple chambers that separate raw materials and help minimize dust, as well as maintaining the integrity of the ingredients. Inside the plant, raw materials are transported throughout the body preparation area by means of special conveyor belts inside closed tubes. These tubes further help control the airborne dust particles that can be an irritating factor in ceramic tile plants.

Extensive recycling of its own materials is also a part of the plant's environmental efforts. Every ceramic tilemaker rejects a percentage of tiles at various steps in production as not meeting established quality standards. At TileCera, these tiles—along with other elements such as waste glaze—are returned to the body preparation area for processing and reuse. In this way, solid waste is virtually eliminated from the manufacturing process. Waste water from the production process is also recycled for other uses in the plant.

Before new tile lines enter production, they are tested in an on-site research and development lab. Located near one end of the building, the lab experiments with new designs and determines performance specifications for all the company's products. The lab includes a small-size press for preparing experimental tile bodies; a variety of jar mills and balances, used in the preparation of experimental glazes; special silkscreening equipment for testing new designs; and a small laboratory kiln, in which technicians can prepare test samples of various tiles. Special equipment tests the expansion characteristics of tile bodies and glazes—critical factors as a tile expands under the intense heat of the kiln and then slowly contracts to its final size.

The performance of both test and actual production samples is analyzed using a variety of lab equipment. A tile-breaking machine tests strength, determining how much stress an individual tile can bear. An autoclave measures how resistant a particular glaze is to crazing, the fine hairline cracks that can develop across a tile's surface. Other tests will determine the tile's water absorption, resistance to slipping, and abrasion resistance. Finally, the lab uses a color difference meter to mathematically determine the precise color and shade of tiles. Technicians make use of a special light booth to examine tiles under different lighting conditions: fluorescent, incandescent, and daylight.

Once tiles have been approved for production, the manufacturing process begins at one extreme end of the plant, in the body preparation area. At this largely automated facility, the combining of various raw materials into the proper clay body mixture is largely controlled by sophisticated computerized machinery, which integrates various aspects of the batching process for maximum efficiency and accuracy. The application software for the process, produces a schematic flow diagram on the screen so that the operator can understand at any point exactly what is going on.

In preparing clay body mixtures, raw products are transported by pneumatic conveyors and mixed according to computer-controlled formulas for the specific type of tile desired. Dry materials and liquids are combined and processed in a large ball mill until the mixture forms small pills or balls, about the size of the lead "shot" in a shotgun shell. Materials in this form (called prills) are then transported to the pressing lines via conveyor belt.

On the pressing line, carefully monitored amounts of prills are injected into special molds and pressed flat under tremendous pressure. The pressing process itself takes less than one second per tile, and the resulting "green" tile is sturdy enough that it can be picked up without losing its shape.

A number of molds are used in each plant, depending on the final size and design of the tile being made. The top surface of the molds may be flat or structured, to provide texture to the finished product. Because this plant specializes in large-format tiles, the presses used here have been specially designed to produce these larger-sized products.

◀ 5 Clay mixtures for TileCera's white-body tiles are prepared in a huge ball mill; the resulting tiny pellets, known as "prills," will be pressed into trim, floor, or wall tiles.

▶ 6 Tiles receive their color and pattern on a 250-foot-long glazing line. For complex stone-look designs, as many as eleven different glazing steps may be required.

Immediately after pressing, tiles are given their color and design on the glazing line. This may be a simple two- or three-step process for a solid-color tile. Other tiles, including stone-look tiles, require multiple decorating steps.

TileCera's glazing line is more than 250 feet long. As tiles move along the line on special conveyor belts, they receive a variety of applications at various types of glazing stations. Virtually all pass first through a curtain of glaze that provides an all-over background color. Designs may be imparted to the entire surface one or more times by means of sophisticated rollers. Multicolor designs are also produced using a series of photographically produced silk screens. Still other stations provide a mist or spray for droplets of additional color.

Once all glazing applications have been completed, tiles are rolled onto specially designed racks. They are held here, often for several hours, until firing.

In its first phase of production, TileCera's plant contains five roller kilns. These state-of-the-art kilns were designed for the facility and specially installed by Sacmi and Nassetti, two of Italy's leading manufacturers of sophisticated ceramic tile technology.

With the modern roller kiln, tiles are moved along metal rollers at a consistent rate of speed through a series of chambers. Heat at each stage is carefully monitored and controlled so that tiles are slowly brought to the proper temperature, held at that temperature for the precise amount of time required by their body and glaze formulas, and then gradually cooled to room temperature. Each stage of the process is equally important. Because tiles actually expand in size under the kiln's intense heat (a maximum of 2192° F), then shrink back as they cool, precise monitoring of temperatures is required at every step. Even minor discrepancies might cause inconsistencies in the tiles' size, shape, and glaze color, as well as in such technical considerations as glaze hardness and water absorption. Somewhat surprisingly, tiles rolling out of the kiln are cool to the touch and may be easily handled for further processing.

Once tiles are completed, they are checked for quality and graded. However, quality is carefully monitored at every stage of the process. Inspectors are stationed along the line to assure that tiles meet rigid quality standards; if not, the tiles are returned to the body preparation area for reuse.

Like all manufacturers, TileCera subjects its products to a number of quality and grading tests. Tiles are sized to assure that they are square and fall within specified size guidelines, and each tile is checked for shading. Visual inspections are made under special lights for pattern and glaze consistency. From each firing, random tiles are selected for laboratory tests to verify overall quality and performance. Finally, those tiles meeting the factory's quality criteria are boxed for shipment to customers.

▲ 7 The finished product: a marble-look glazed floor tile in black. Multiple glazing steps, including a special silkscreen to produce the naturalistic veins, are required to produce this tile.

Handcrafted Tile Factory Tour: Stellar Ceramics

The distinction between handcrafted and machinemade tile becomes most evident when touring a factory producing handcrafted tile. Stellar Ceramics, located in the wine country north of San Francisco, demonstrates this hands-on approach to the manufacture of both terra cotta and white bisque handcrafted tiles.

Incorporated in January 1991, Stellar first researched market trends and, as a result, developed a product line of carved relief tiles using an extensive color palette. Custom capabilities are also an important aspect of the company's offerings.

Upon entering the factory, you immediately notice the labor intensity of Stellar's manufacturing process. At each stage of operation, the product is handled by people, not machines. Each piece of tile is handled no less than ten times, thereby encouraging handmade nuances in the product. Even the manufacturing equipment, including the 96-cubic-foot firing kilns, were built on-site by Stellar employees.

Because of the emphasis on both handcrafted and custom designs, production naturally evolves from the design department. Designs are sculpted from plasticene, an oil-based clay, and molds are created by pouring plaster over the design. After the plaster has hardened, the plasticene is dug out

▶ 8 A large relief tile is pressed from wet clay using a ram-press equipped with a custom-made die.

and the mold is cleaned. Clay is then pressed by hand into the mold to create the first casting of the new design. Compressed air is used to extract the first sample tile, and the design is then reviewed by the designer and the sales department. Once the design is approved, sample tiles are pounded out from the mold, glazed, and fired. With most new designs, customer input is sought before the design is cast into a die.

Die making is the next step, with all dies made in-house. First, plaster casts are made of the mold to create a master record of the design, then dies are created from the plaster casts. These dies, also made of plaster, are used to form the size, shape, and design of the tiles during production. They are equipped with an air tubing system to allow for quick release of the clay from the die following each pressing.

Two ram-presses, equipped with these custom-made dies, are used to produce both flat and relief tiles. Moist clay is pugged (kneaded) through vacuum de-airing pug mills and pressed into the dies under 25 tons of pressure. The relief tiles require an additional step since they must be hand-trimmed, checked for flaws and touched up while the clay is still wet. Both flat and relief tiles are then placed on carts in preparation for the drying tunnel. Under the best conditions, a single press can produce 400 square feet of tile per shift with a single operator.

All moldings of linear design are extruded by a hydraulic extruder also built in-house. The extruder can produce up to 1000 linear feet of moldings per shift. The extrusion dies (patent pending) provide an air cushion around the clay as it is forced through the die, a process that eliminates dragging and tearing of the clay. The moldings are then placed on carts and wrapped in plastic to reduce warping.

▲ 9 After pressing, scrap clay is hand-trimmed from the relief tiles.

◀ 10 Glaze firing begins after the tiles, placed on setters, are loaded into the kiln. The three pyrometric cones will melt when firing is complete.

All carts of wet tiles are subsequently rolled into the entry of a 40-foot-long drying tunnel. Inside the tunnel, warm air is pushed in from one side and cooler, moist air is pulled out from the other side. The moist air is then dehumidified and heated before reentering the tunnel. Normal drying cycles are from 8 to 12 hours, depending on the product. Following drying, the tiles are inspected, cleaned, and loaded onto self-stacking, high-refractory content shelves, called saggars, in preparation for bisque firing.

The firing of the simple box-shaped kiln is manually controlled by the firemaster of the current shift who determines the placement of the saggars, rate of climb of temperature, gas, and damper adjustments, and many other factors affecting the firing. Since the process is an approximate art, a degree of inconsistency occurs, contributing to the subtle variation in the finished product. The tiles are then cooled and stored in preparation for glazing.

▲ 11 The end result: handcrafted relief wall tiles and moldings. Tiles are handled by people, not machines, thereby encouraging handmade nuances in the product.

Stellar's glazing process is also very labor-intensive. Tiles are loaded on racks, hand sprayed, and then weighed on an electronic gram scale to determine the precise amount of glaze added to the tile. Each tile is periodically weighed again until the desired spray weight has been achieved. The terra cotta tiles require an additional step since, before applying the colored glaze, an undercoat must first be applied and allowed to dry.

During and after spraying, special care is taken to recycle materials and address environmental concerns associated with this aspect of the manufacturing process. First, the spray booth is designed with sloping sides to direct the overspray to a container for reuse. Second, the racks are ventilated so that air can be drawn through them in a downdraft. This helps to reduce turbulence around the spray booth and airborne particulate is removed almost instantly. The air is then pulled to the bottom of the spray booth and directed to a continuously recirculating water-wash filter to capture any remaining particulate before exiting the building. Finally, special care is taken to recycle the overspray left on the glazing racks.

Glaze firing is a most important step, since mistakes here could jeopardize the work of the entire crew that has brought the tile to this stage. The firemaster's skill is utilized to determine the placement of tile in the 96-cubic-foot gas-fired envelope kiln. Then, the firemaster carefully directs the firing—monitoring the rise in temperature, adjusting the dampers, and recording the progress on the firing log. Pyrometric cones, or tapered triangular-shaped pieces of material designed to melt at certain temperatures, tell the firemaster when the firing is complete. Normally, the glaze firing cycle is complete in about $7^{1}/_{2}$ hours. Subsequently, the tiles are cooled for approximately 8 to 10 hours.

Once tiles are completed, a final quality control inspection is made prior to packaging. Color standards are checked; flawed tiles are separated. First-class tiles are vacuum-sealed and boxed for shipment.

Applications

The versatility of ceramic tile lends itself to use in many spaces and surfaces within a home. This has been demonstrated by the Europeans, since tile is commonly used not only in kitchens and baths, but throughout the home in living rooms, dining rooms, bedrooms, and patios. The Ceramic Tile Distributors Association (CTDA) International Council reports that the per capita use of ceramic tile in Italy is more than ten times that of the United States.

▲ 12 This once plain breakfast room has undergone a transformation by adding a tile "area rug" beneath the dining table. The custom tile design was premounted onto sheets at the factory using glazed mosaics in squares, triangles, and liners.

Why, then, is tile considered to be a superior choice? And where is it appropriate to use tile in a home?

Ceramic tile is a superior choice because its life-cycle costs are lower than those for most other finish materials—carpet, vinyl, paint, plastic laminates, terrazzo, and marble. Although initial material and installation costs are sometimes higher, ceramic tile is the most economical for the life of the material. In a study conducted for TCA by the cost-consulting firm of Robin S. Godfrey, Inc., ceramic tile and other common finish materials were evaluated over a 40-year span. Installation, maintenance, and replacement costs were determined and compared. Both ceramic wall and floor tile were found to have the lowest annual cost per square foot.

In addition, tiles are a superior finish material since they have a beauty and timelessness that enhances the character of a house. Featureless tract houses, typically finished with nondescript floor vinyl, carpet, and plastic laminates are transformed when these finishes are replaced with beautiful and enduring ceramic tiles. Even the most bland, characterless rooms can be imbued with a feeling of permanence and style with the imaginative use of tile. The effect is even tangible, since resale values increase when ceramic tile is installed in remodeled homes.

Tile can be used on almost any surface and in any room in a home as long as the substrate is appropriate and structurally sound. Options include floors, walls, ceilings, and countertops in kitchens, baths, entries, living rooms, dining rooms, and bedrooms, as well as garages, patios, and walkways. Thought must be given to the total design aesthetic and to factors such as hygiene, durability, and maintenance so that tile can be employed where it is most needed. Here are some questions to consider when selecting finish materials:

1. Is hygiene a factor?
2. How durable and permanent should this finish be?
3. Is ornament, texture, or color needed?
4. What are the maintenance factors?
5. How can I best give character to the room?
6. Do I want the space to have a enduring quality?
7. What is my budget for initial and life-cycle costs?
8. What materials best fit the total design?

We will look more closely at these questions in later chapters, but it should become apparent that there are many, many applications where tile is the most appropriate and best choice.

Floors

Ceramic tile is well suited to the special demands of floors. For durability under foot traffic, resistance to moisture, and ease of maintenance, few materials can match its performance. Even the impact of high heeled shoes or the occasional mishap with mud or food spills will not harm ceramic floor tile. Cleanup is easy with a neutral cleaner and a damp mop.

In addition to its functionality, ceramic floor tiles add beauty and a feeling of permanence to a room. They may be used as either the decorative focus or as a backdrop to other finishes, depending on the type, color, and pattern selected. Many different moods and styles can be created using floor tiles. Since the character of the floor sets the tone of the room more than any other single surface, ceramic floor tile can have significant impact on the design.

◄ 13 The relaxed ambiance of this entry hall is derived from the casual look of the blue, glazed floor tiles. Durability and ease of cleaning are additional benefits of the use of tile in this high traffic area.

▲ 14 This interesting installation utilizes several sizes of glazed tiles to highlight the plate shelf and to sheath the lower portion of the wall.

Walls

Walls provide an opportunity for especially interesting and dramatic applications of ceramic tile. Since foot traffic is not a factor, the softer, more easily scratched, high-gloss, and intensely colored glazes can be used to provide dramatic effect. Whether a decorative accent or focal point, ceramic wall tiles have the ability to transform and enliven a colorless or nondescript room.

Application of ceramic tile to walls also provides a durable, hygienic, and low maintenance alternative to paint or wall paper. Its advantages are especially apparent for areas subject to water or grease. Glazed tile works particularly well in high-maintenance areas, such as kitchens and baths.

Countertops

Both function and aesthetics are well-served when countertops are finished with ceramic tile. Whether in the kitchen, bath, dressing area, or bar, ceramic tile countertops can provide an impervious work surface that resists moisture, stains, alcohol, scratching, and excessive temperature. No other finish material offers this level of durability economically. In fact, only certain types of natural granite, at considerable additional expense, can match the performance characteristics of ceramic tile for countertops.

Decorative impact is easily achieved with ceramic tile countertops. Patterns, textures, and colors can be creatively combined and applied to the countertop or backsplash. It is often desirable to continue the countertop pattern or color to the backsplash; however, you may want a solid color countertop with a patterned or accent color backsplash.

▶ 15-16 A hand-painted tile mural and coordinated edge trim grace the backsplash and countertop in this lovely kitchen. Monochromatic white tile is used on the countertop itself in order to avoid cluttering the work surface.

A quick word about grout is in order here since it becomes a critical factor where stains are likely. Because grout manufacturers have made significant improvements in recent years, there are several good choices available. A 100 percent solids epoxy grout is an excellent choice for countertops since it is impervious to water and stains. (Chapter 7 provides a detailed description of the available options.)

Fireplaces

Fireplaces provide a unique opportunity to employ the heat resistant characteristics of ceramic tile. Because of their tolerance of heat, ceramic tile may be installed at the hearth, on the outside face or inner edge, providing both a functional and aesthetic solution. Many American colonial homes use a single row of tile on the fireplace face. This technique is still popular and provides an excellent opportunity to display decorative or antique tiles.

► 17 Handcrafted sculptural relief tiles were used to create this custom fireplace facade.

Stretcher

▲ 18 Since not all fireplaces are the same, stretcher tiles can be used to accommodate an odd-size opening by centering the oversized stretcher tile in the space and cutting the appropriate amount from the left and right sides.

Exteriors

Ceramic tile is an excellent way to enhance an exterior space, such as a patio, walkway, swimming pool, or spa. Tile makes a patio feel more like an exterior room, giving it a natural and inviting warmth that stark gray concrete cannot imbue. It also makes an entrance walkway inviting with the creative use of mosaic patterns, porcelain pavers, or earth-toned quarry tiles. Colorful decorative tiles give life to pools and fountains by highlighting the waterline with deep blues and greens.

◀ 19 Tile turns a plain concrete walkway into an avenue of enduring beauty. This installation features a unique porcelain paver tile with an antiqued look.

◀ 20 Terra cotta is a favorite choice for stair treads since it provides durability and good slip resistance.

The selection of a frost-resistant tile is extremely important for exterior use in freeze-thaw climates. Most porcelain mosaics and pavers, as well as some quarry tiles meet this requirement, but it is important to check with the manufacturer before purchase. Even though some varieties are frost-resistant, most glazed tiles are not recommended for exterior use on any horizontal surface subject to foot traffic. This is due to the increased possibility of slipping when glazed tiles are wet.

Stairs

Although they have different usage requirements, both stair treads and stair risers can benefit from the application of ceramic tile. Stair treads can especially benefit from the durability and slip resistance of ceramic tile. Some manufacturers even offer special stair tread tiles with ribbed nosings and bullnosed edges. These provide both a functional and attractive solution. Stair risers are less subject to wear, and provide an excellent opportunity to display decorative glazed tiles. This technique also increases safety, since it helps make each step more visible.

Types of Tile

Ceramic tile improves the quality of our lives by adding interest and variety to the built environment. Such enhancement is made possible thanks to the myriad of colors, shapes, sizes, and textures of ceramic tile available today. From high-gloss, glazed wall tile to unglazed porcelain pavers, mosaics, quarry tiles, and handmade terra cotta floor tiles, the options are seemingly endless.

In order to simplify the range of choices, ceramic tile is often categorized into groups or types of tile. Tiles are usually grouped according to their finish surface, material composition, or manufacturing method. One very important way to group tiles is by their ability to absorb water. This is a characteristic that applies only to the body of the tile, not the glaze. The amount of water a tile body absorbs can determine its appropriateness for exterior use in freeze-thaw climates and its wear properties and density. Tiles with low levels of absorption are usually more frost resistant, durable, longer-wearing, and stain resistant than the more porous types.

The American National Standard Specifications for Ceramic Tile (ANSI A137.1) classifies the water absorption of ceramic tile in four groups:

1. *Impervious*—Tile with water absorption of 0.5 percent or less.

2. *Vitreous*—Tile with water absorption of more than 0.5 percent, but no more than 3 percent.

▲ 21 The earth's natural striations are depicted in this buff-colored quarry tile, adding a natural ambiance to this foyer and living room. The use of squares and picket shapes adds additional interest to the floor.

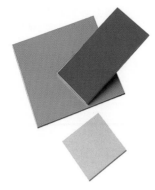

Matte

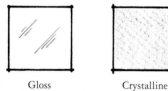

Gloss   Crystalline

Textured   Decorative

▲ 22 Glazed wall tiles.

▲ 23 Typical glaze types of glazed wall tiles.

3. *Semivitreous*—Tile with water absorption of more than 3 percent, but no more than 7 percent.

4. *Nonvitreous*—Tile with water absorption of more than 7 percent.

These terms are important in understanding ceramic tile, and they will be used throughout this book.

With regard to quality, ceramic tile is defined by ANSI A137.1 into two major groups: standard grade and second grade. Standard grade is the highest quality and is used for most applications. Second grade allows certain facial defects and may be used if warranted by budget constraints.

The following sections provide a detailed description of the most common types of ceramic tile. Tips for identifying tiles, manufacturing methods, and physical characteristics are included, as well as a discussion of appropriate areas for use. The most commonly available sizes, shapes, colors, and textures are also provided.

Glazed Wall Tile

The term glazed wall tile is used to describe tiles that are usually nonvitreous, with light-duty bodies and relatively soft, impervious glazes applied to the surface. They are not required or expected to withstand excessive impact or be subject to freeze-thaw conditions. Glazed wall tiles are sometimes known as white body tiles because of their easily identifiable white body. They are manufactured by the dust-pressed method, making them uniform and consistent in appearance. They are also economical, require minimal maintenance, and are easy to install due to the existence of spacer lugs on many varieties.

As the name suggests, glazed wall tiles are suitable for most wall applications in both residential and commercial settings. However, they are not always limited to wall use. Some manufacturers of glazed wall tiles recommend their use on certain light-duty floors, such as residential bathrooms. Be sure to check with the manufacturer to determine if their wall tiles are suitable for this type of floor use.

Glazed wall tiles have significant limitations for use due to the characteristics of both their body and glaze. First, the body of most glazed wall tiles is usually nonvitreous and therefore not frost-resistant. This fact limits their use to interiors in most climates. Also, the body has a relatively low breaking strength, which limits their use to walls in all but the most light-duty flooring applications. Second, most wall tile glazes cannot withstand heavy foot traffic, as it would scratch and wear through to the body.

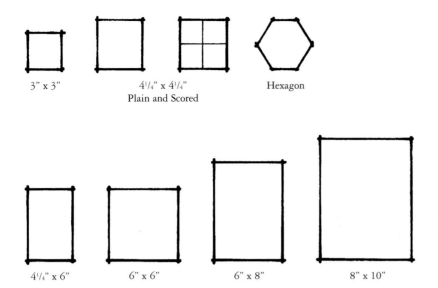

3" x 3"

4¹/₄" x 4¹/₄"
Plain and Scored

Hexagon

4¹/₄" x 6"

6" x 6"

6" x 8"

8" x 10"

◄ 24 Typical sizes and shapes of glazed wall tile.

Additionally, these glazes are often slick and do not provide the slip resistance required for use on commercial floors.

The real beauty of glazed wall tiles stems from their colorful surface glaze, whether it is gloss, semigloss, matte, or textured. Glazed wall tiles are manufactured in an enormous variety of colors, with coordinating decorative tiles, molding, and trim shapes. Some manufacturers provide sizes that are modular, allowing for creative patterning of these colorful tiles. Other manufacturers provide colors that match plumbing fixtures, allowing for a color-coordinated design in kitchens and baths.

Historically, the most common nominal sizes include 3" x 3", 4¹/₄" x 4¹/₄", 4¹/₄" x 6", and 6" x 6". More recently, 6" x 8", 8" x 10", and larger sizes have also gained popularity. The typical nominal thickness is ⁵/₁₆". Spacer lugs typically allow for a uniform ¹/₁₆" grout line.

Ceramic Mosaic Tile

Ceramic mosaics are small tiles made of porcelain or natural clay. These small tiles are factory-mounted on the back, face, or edge with paper, thread mesh, or polyvinyl chloride onto one or two square foot sheets. Usually, ceramic mosaics are manufactured by the dust-pressed method. Depending on the manufacturer, they are either impervious or vitreous. Ceramic mosaics are available in both glazed and unglazed varieties and in several shapes, including squares, rectangles, and hexagons.

Unglazed ceramic mosaics are extremely durable and can be used for all types of floor and wall applications, including kitchens, bathrooms, shower

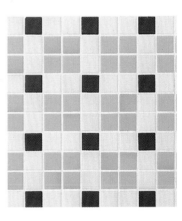

▲ 25 Ceramic mosaic tiles set in a pattern.

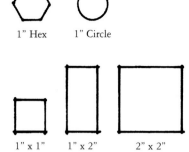

1" Hex   1" Circle

1" x 1"   1" x 2"   2" x 2"

▲ 26 Typical sizes and shapes of ceramic mosaic tile.

floors, and swimming pools. Since they are unglazed, they also provide good slip resistance for most uses. They can also be manufactured with an abrasive particle added to the body of the tile. This abrasive additive provides a higher coefficient of friction, which may be necessary in certain wet areas, such as the floor of tiled mud rooms, and showers. Depending on the manufacturer, most unglazed ceramic mosaics are also frost-resistant, making them suitable for exterior use on patios, walkways, fountains, swimming pools, and building facades.

The appropriate use of glazed ceramic mosaics varies widely, depending on the type of glaze. Generally, the shinier the glaze, the more easily the tile can be scratched. Therefore, in most cases, shiny glazes should be installed on walls only. Many matte finish glazes are suitable for residential floor use; however, this information should be verified with the manufacturer.

Ceramic mosaics, in both glazed and unglazed varieties, are perhaps the most versatile type of tile. They are manufactured in a wide range of colors, sizes, and shapes that can be factory mounted into patterns. This unique characteristic allows for customized patterns that are both economical and easy to install. Some well-known patterns include the Greek key, random, and checkerboard patterns. Original, custom designs are also easily manufactured. Often, ceramic mosaics are modular, allowing for the use of two or three different sizes within a custom pattern.

Typical nominal sizes of ceramic mosaics include 1" x 1", 1" x 2", and 2" x 2". The typical nominal thickness is $1/4$".

GLAZED MOSAICS

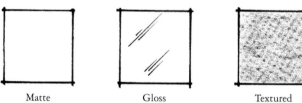

Matte   Gloss   Textured

UNGLAZED MOSAICS

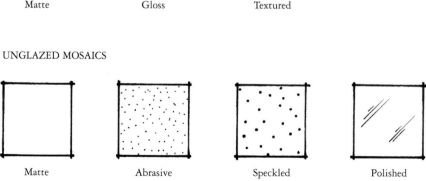

Matte   Abrasive   Speckled   Polished

▶ 27 Types of ceramic mosaic tile.

Quarry Tile

The term quarry tile is used to describe tiles manufactured by the extrusion process. In this process, the tile is shaped by forcing plastic clay or shale through a die that results in their distinctive, natural appearance. After extrusion, the tile is fired and sometimes glazed.

Although unglazed quarry tiles are among the most economical and durable choices for floor materials, they are also suitable for walls and countertops. Their distinctive coloring usually comes from the inherent color of their natural clay or shale body. Unglazed quarry tiles are unique since the manufacturing process produces a surface skin that is less absorptive than the body of the tile. This surface skin results in improved stain resistance and with time, develops a patina that adds to the beauty of these tiles. Some manufacturers provide a variation on the unglazed quarry tiles in which the tiles are precision-ground after firing. This variation produces a natural clay tile that is very uniform in dimension. Unglazed quarry tiles provide good slip resistance for most flooring applications. Some are also available with an abrasive particle, but this is generally only needed in special applications where improved slip resistance is required.

Most glazed quarry tiles are durable enough for floor use, as well as for walls and countertops. They are particularly suited for areas where ease of maintenance is a priority, since the impervious glaze protects the tile from stains. Glazed quarry tiles are generally more expensive than unglazed quarry tiles, since an additional step is performed in the manufacturing process.

▲ 28 Quarry tiles.

UNGLAZED QUARRY

Natural

Flashed

Wood Grain

Abraisive

GLAZED QUARRY

Semi-gloss

Matte

Speckled

Abrasive

◀ 29 Types of quarry tile.

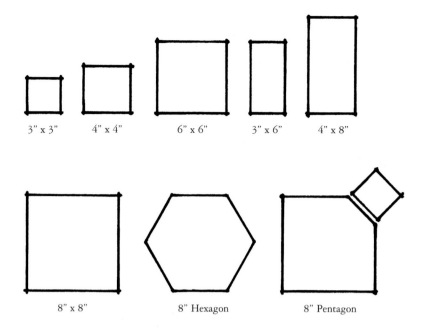

3" x 3"   4" x 4"   6" x 6"   3" x 6"   4" x 8"

8" x 8"   8" Hexagon   8" Pentagon

In appropriate applications this added cost is offset by both the ease of maintenance and striking beauty of the colorful surface glaze.

Because some quarry tiles are frost-resistant while others are not, you should always check with the manufacturer before installing them outdoors. The unglazed frost-resistant quarry tiles are an excellent choice for exterior patios and walkways: they are very durable, are inherently slip-resistant, and add a warm earthy ambiance to these surfaces. The glazed frost-resistant types can be used on exterior vertical surfaces, such as facades or planters. Since slipping could occur, they should not be used on pedestrian walkways.

Unglazed quarry tiles derive their color from the tile's body composition and are generally earthy reds, tans, browns, or grays. Some manufacturers have produced a wider range of unglazed colors including muted blues, greens, and pinks. For more dramatic color, glazed quarry tiles provide an extensive palate of gloss and matte glazes. The glazes are often quite intense and can include vibrant blues, greens, mauves, purples, and reds.

Typical nominal sizes include 4" x 8", 6" x 6", 8" x 8", and 8" hexagons. The typical nominal thicknesses are $^3/_8$", or $^1/_2$". Some manufacturers may offer quarry tiles in $^3/_4$" thickness.

Paver Tile

Manufactured by the dust-pressed method, paver tiles are larger tiles made of porcelain or natural clay. Paver tiles are often confused with quarry tiles because they are similar in size, weight, and suitability for heavy-duty floor

▲ 31 Porcelain paver tiles shown in natural, slate, and grid finishes.

use. Paver tiles are, nevertheless, distinct from quarry tiles because of the large variety of colors and finishes available. They occur in glazed and unglazed types and most are either impervious or vitreous.

The composition and physical characteristics of unglazed porcelain paver tiles are similar to those of unglazed porcelain mosaics. Like porcelain mosaics, they are extremely durable and can be used for most floors and walls in both interior and exterior applications. However, unlike porcelain mosaics, they are manufactured in larger sizes and with different surface textures that provide varied appearances and levels of slip resistance. Typical surface textures include natural, slate, polished, and sandblasted, as well as various raised-grid patterns. The sandblasted and grid finishes provide the highest levels of slip resistance, whereas the polished finish can be slippery, especially when wet.

The performance characteristics of glazes for glazed paver tiles are usually significantly different from those of glazes applied to glazed wall tiles. The two should not be confused. While most glazes for wall tiles are relatively soft and more easily scratched, many glazed pavers have a very hard glaze that is durable enough for even the heaviest commercial foot traffic. Tests such as the Moh's scale of hardness and the Abrasive

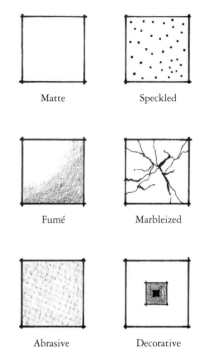

Matte   Speckled

Fumé   Marbleized

Abrasive   Decorative

▲ 32 Typical glaze types of glazed paver tiles.

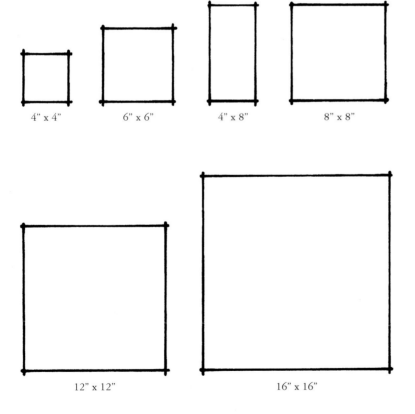

4" x 4"   6" x 6"   4" x 8"   8" x 8"

12" x 12"   16" x 16"

◀ 33 Typical sizes and shapes of paver tile.

Wear Index for Glazed Floor Tile (ASTM C 1027) are helpful in determining the hardness and durability of these floor-use glazes. (A description of these tests is in Appendix 4.) In addition to durability, glazed paver tiles are very easy to maintain since the impervious, glasslike glaze protects the tile from stains.

Once installed, the appearance of some glazed and unglazed paver tiles is similar, and it is sometimes difficult to discern between the two types. Both glazed and unglazed pavers come in solid and speckled colors; the matte glazed tiles closely match the appearance of the natural finish unglazed tiles. Large-scale patterns are easily achieved by combining two or more colors of paver tiles or by combining solid color tiles with speckled tiles. Many varieties are also modular, allowing for several sizes to be patterned together. Patterns are often developed using 12" x 12" and 6" x 6" tiles or 12" x 12", 8" x 8", and 4" x 8" tiles.

Typical nominal sizes are 8" x 8" and 12" x 12". Other sizes include 4" x 4", 4" x 8", 6" x 6", 6" x 12", 16" x 16", and 24" x 24". The typical nominal thickness is 5/16".

Terra Cotta Tile

Made from natural clays, terra cotta tiles have a charming, old-world appearance that is distinctive. This old-world appearance is achieved through subtle variations in color, texture, shape, and size. Variation can occur from tile to tile or within an individual tile, and imperfections are considered desirable. Because of their high absorption rate and nonvitreous classification, terra cotta tiles are not resistant to frost, and should not be used outdoors in freeze-thaw climates. Also, these absorptive characteristics usually require that sealers be applied to prevent stains and to increase the wearability of these soft clay tiles. Sealers may be either factory- or field-applied. Periodic reapplication is often necessary.

Terra cotta tiles are used mainly for floors because of their thick, heavy body. They range in color from reds and browns to tans and yellows. Pigmented stains can be used to alter the natural color, as with the whitewashed varieties. The application of a sealer usually intensifies the stained or inherent color and gives the tile shine. Several shapes are available, including squares, rectangles, hexagons, octagons, and various contoured designs.

Mexican floor tiles, or Saltillo tiles, are a unique type of terra cotta tile handmade in Mexico using time-honored techniques. Clay is obtained from the region surrounding Saltillo, Mexico, blended with water, molded, dried, and fired at low temperatures. Occasionally a dog or chicken print can be found on the surface. This occurs when an animal happens to stray across the tile drying in the sun.

▲ 34 Terra cotta tiles.

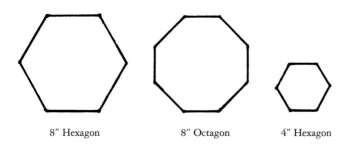

8" Hexagon   8" Octagon   4" Hexagon

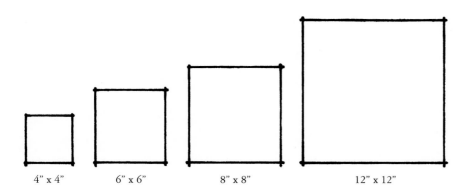

4" x 4"   6" x 6"   8" x 8"   12" x 12"

Typical nominal sizes range from 4" x 4" up to 12" x 12". The thickness is irregular and generally ranges between $^3/_4$" to 1". Because of this irregularity, special consideration should be given to the setting method, commonly a mortar bed installation. (See Chapter 7 for a description of this installation method.)

Other Tiles

There are several additional types of tile that merit brief mention. These are glass mosaics, decorative tile, decorative thin wall tile, faience tiles, and ceramic murals.

Glass Mosaics

Glass mosaics are small tiles made of glass. As with ceramic mosaics, they are mounted on sheets, usually of paper, that are 12" square. Both squares, or Venetian mosaics, and irregularly cut shapes, or Byzantine mosaics, are produced. They may be used monochromatically or in multicolored patterns or murals.

▲ 36 Glass mosaic tiles.

▲ 37

▲ 38

▲ 39

▲ 40

Decorative Tiles

▲ 37-44 Decorative tiles are available in a wide variety of styles as shown in this sampling.

Decorative tiles are tiles with pattern, ornament, or decoration on their surface. They may be glazed or unglazed, and can be handmade or machine-produced. Sometimes their designs are embossed or formed in relief. Flowers, birds, and geometric designs are common motifs. Often decorative tiles are color coordinated with a monochromatic line of glazed wall tiles.

▲ 41

▲ 42

▲ 43

▲ 44

Decorative Thin Wall Tile

Decorative thin wall tiles are very thin, glazed wall tiles that are only intended for light-use wall applications. These tiles meet all the ANSI requirements for regular glazed wall tile except in the area of breaking strength. When installed, the appearance of these tiles is the same as that of glazed wall tiles, but they are generally less expensive.

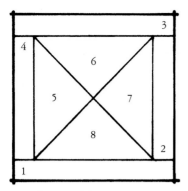

Customized Decorative Tile

▲ 45 This type of glazed decorative tile follows a standardized pattern but allows for custom placement of up to eight glaze colors.

Faience Tiles

Faience tiles are tiles that have variations in the face, edges, and glaze that give the appearance of a handmade product. These variations may be present within a single tile or from tile to tile. Faience tiles may be glazed or unglazed, and are manufactured in a wide range of sizes.

Ceramic Tile Murals

Ceramic tile murals combine several tiles to create pictures or scenes. They may be created in many ways. One method uses relatively large tiles that have portions of the total design painted or silk screened on each tile. The tiles are then fitted together in the proper order and installed. Another method uses many multicolored mosaics to create the picture. The result is an abstracted, patchwork appearance. Usually, mosaic murals are created in the factory and shipped to the job site on 1' x 2' sheets. The sheets are then fitted together in the proper order to form the design.

▲ 46 Hand-painted mural and coordinated decorative tiles.

Choosing Tiles

Because of ceramic tile's innate beauty, the selection process is often affected by a strong attraction to a particular tile. Perhaps one is immediately drawn to the intensity of a glaze, or to a unique decorative pattern. Or you may be attracted to a certain color that particularly suits your needs.

While this method has its merits and place within the total selection process, the decision should not be based solely on aesthetics. Instead, the attraction to a particular tile should be backed by a thorough analysis and understanding of all the factors that have impact on the success of the installation. This includes factors such as durability, slip resistance, frost resistance, and maintenance. This analysis is especially important because of the permanency of tile installations. Mistakes can be expensive and not always easily remedied after tile is installed.

Durability

The durability of various ceramic tiles must be considered when selecting tile for most applications. Foot traffic, even in residential applications, can damage certain ceramic tiles if they are not structurally suitable or appropriately glazed to meet this demand. Because knives and other sharp kitchen utensils can scratch some glazed ceramic tiles, durability must be considered when selecting kitchen countertop tiles. Even some walls, especially in industrial and commercial applications, can have severe service requirements that necessitate an informed selection of durable ceramic tiles.

The first step toward selecting an appropriately durable tile is to evaluate the level of wear that the installation will be subjected to. Floor applications generally carry the heaviest wear and can be subjected to various levels of foot traffic, impact loads, heat, stains, or the wheels of heavily loaded carts. The Tile Council of America rates floor performance level requirements as extra heavy, heavy, moderate, light, and residential. (Appendix 2 identifies these categories and the types of buildings and spaces associated with each.) Some countertops maybe subjected to acids, sharp objects, food stains, and scratching. Because kitchen countertops have high levels of wear, tiles should be carefully selected based on the manufacturers recommendations for this use.

After determining the wear requirement, the next step is to evaluate and select tiles with wear properties that meet this demand. The first and most important method of deciding if a particular tile is right for your installation is to know the tile manufacturer's recommendation for its use. In fact, it is often not necessary to research the test results, since the manufacturer's recommendation is sufficient. You should never disregard the manufacturer's recommendation for use, since undesirable consequences are likely and the warranty would be void. Tile breakage, chipping, and unsightly wearing of the glaze can be the long-term results of inappropriate use.

Because several tiles may be recommended as sufficiently durable for your particular installation, the choice is up to you. In this case, comparison of the ASTM test results can assist in making a final selection, if you want to select the tile that rates highest for durability. Specific test results for wearability, breaking strength, and abrasion resistance are of particular importance—ASTM C 501, C 648, and C 1027, test for these qualities. (A description of these and other common test methods is provided in Appendix 4.)

The selection of glazed tiles requires special consideration to determine the hardness and wearability of the surface glaze. There have been significant advances in the manufacture of glazes in recent years. Many are suitable for floor use, but you must be careful to follow the manufacturer's recommendations for use. Most high-gloss and intensely colored glazes are relatively soft and should be eliminated from floor use, unless the manufacturer specifically permits this use. However, some glazed tiles are very long-wearing and are available with 10- to 20-year warranties. Test results that assist in determining the durability of glazes are ASTM C 1027 (also known as the Abrasive Wear Index for Glazed Floor Tile), and Moh's scale of hardness. Some manufacturers of glazed floor tiles suggest that a safe guideline for heavy traffic usage is to follow minimum standards for these tests as follows:

Abrasive Wear Index—3 minimum

Moh's scale—7 minimum

(See Appendix 4 for a description of these test methods.)

Slip Resistance

The slip resistance of flooring is increasingly important in our litigious society and should be considered when choosing tiles for use in pedestrian traffic areas in both residential and commercial applications. The National Safety Council estimates that within a 12-month period, approximately 12 million persons in the United States are injured seriously enough in falls to require at least one day of restricted activity. Many of these accidents result in lawsuits filed against the property owner or design professional.

Careful consideration of the slip resistance of floor tile can help to prevent accidents. Common locations for slipping in the home are in bathrooms, entryways, kitchens, swimming pool decks, and exterior walkways. The common factor in all these locations is water, since most walking surfaces tend to become slippery when wet. In kitchens, grease and water can combine to create dangerously slippery conditions if proper maintenance is not performed.

The test method commonly used to evaluate the coefficient of friction or slip resistance of ceramic tile is ASTM C 1028. In this test method, neolite, a common shoe sole and heel material, is pulled across the surface of both a wet and dry tile using a dynamometer pull meter. The recorded measurements indicate the level of resistance to slipping present. These measurements are known as the static coefficient of friction (s.c.o.f.). Depending on the conditions, the static coefficient of friction can range between 0.1 and 0.9 or higher. The higher the number, the more slip resistant the surface. (See Appendix 4 for a more detailed description of ASTM C 1028.)

While this test method is in common use by the tile industry, there is no nationally recognized standard for slip resistance, nor has a test method been adopted by ANSI A137.1. This is due, in part, to discrepencies in the various test methods available and the controversies surrounding this issue. Moreover, the Americans with Disabilities Act (ADA) has not mandated a standard value for static coefficient of friction, requiring only that accessible routes be stable, firm, and slip-resistant. In addition the ADA states that "in its simplest sense, a slip-resistant surface is one that will permit an individual to walk across it without slipping." Still, the ADA does include advisory recommendations for static coefficient of friction derived from research performed using a silastic sensor in lieu of neolite. These advisory recommendations are as follows:

0.6 s.c.o.f. for floors (on accessible routes)

0.8 s.c.o.f. for ramps (on accessible routes)

Similarly, the Occupational Safety and Health Administration (OSHA) has not mandated a static coefficient of friction, but recommends 0.5 s.c.o.f. as the minimum to prevent slipping.

Unfortunately, it is difficult to interpret and compare these recommendations since different test methods and sensors were used from those typically used to test ceramic tile. However, they can serve as a general guide in evaluating a tile's slip resistance relative to its proposed installation site.

Manufacturers supply tiles with a range of slip resistance, and many meet the recommended levels listed above. Abrasive particles are sometimes added to either the body or glaze of the tile to increase its slip resistance.

Other tiles, such as unglazed, sculptured, and sandblasted, have characteristics that are inherently slip-resistant.

Mistakes regarding slip resistance are not easily remedied because of the permanence of tile installations. Acid etching or special slip-resistant coatings can be applied to increase the coefficient of friction of glazed and unglazed tile. These remedies are not always successful and usually require periodic reapplication.

It is important to note that while slip-resistant tiles have significant benefits, they also can be more difficult to clean. In general, the more slip-resistant the tile, the more likely it is to retain dirt. The additional maintenance that results is sometimes unsatisfactory to the owner. Therefore, a balanced approach is recommended where slip resistance, maintenance, and aesthetics are considered of equal importance.

Lastly, maintenance obviously plays an important role in the safety of walking surfaces. Even highly textured floors will be slippery if proper maintenance is not followed and grease is allowed to sit on the surface of the tile. In some cases, tile installations may require the use of a wet-vac to thoroughly remove the grease and properly maintain a slip-resistant floor.

Resistance to Freezing

When selecting tile for outdoor use, one must be careful to consider the climate that the tile will be subjected to. Climatic conditions such as blowing sand, rain, hail, and snow should all be evaluated for their effect on the installation. This is especially true for climates that undergo freeze-thaw cycles, since this process is destructive to many types of porous ceramic tile. Specifically, this process involves the penetration of water into the body of the tile, water that is then frozen during the winter months. Because water expands when it freezes, the tile is forced to crack, chip, or spall.

To avoid this unfortunate scenario, select a tile that resists the penetration of water and is recommended by the manufacturer for this application. Tiles that are impervious or vitreous have low absorption rates, and therefore generally meet this criterion. Tiles that are classified as semivitreous or nonvitreous have higher absorption rates and, unless recommended by the manufacturer, should not be used outdoors in freeze-thaw climates. (See Appendix 3.)

There are several methods of determining the frost resistance of ceramic tile. These methods include the recommendations of the tile manufacturer, as well as the review of test results for both water absorption and frost resistance. These tests are described in ASTM C 373 and ASTM C 1026 respectively. (They are described in Appendix 4.) Another method of determining frost resistance is to review existing exterior installations of the particular tile you are considering. Usually, the tile manufacturer can provide you with these project references.

Maintenance Factors

Ease of cleaning and maintenance is one of the positive characteristics of ceramic tile. Tile resists water, grease, dirt, and food stains, and is the material of choice for kitchens and baths. It is, however, a misconception to think that ceramic tile is maintenance-free. There are different levels of maintenance available depending on the type of tile.

Glazed tiles are usually the easiest types of tile to clean and maintain. Glazed tiles are protected from dirt and stains by the impervious surface glaze. The glaze acts like a sheet of glass, completely covering and protecting the surface of the tile. Because water, grease, dirt, and food cannot penetrate the glaze, they can easily be wiped away. Both glazed floor tiles and glazed wall tiles are easily cleaned using warm water and a neutral cleaner.

Unglazed tiles may not be as easy to keep clean, since the surface is unprotected. Still, dark unglazed tiles and brown or red quarry tiles are relatively easy to maintain since stains and dirt do not show. Light colored unglazed tiles require additional care because they can show surface dirt and stains. Dense unglazed tiles are usually more stain-resistant than the relatively porous types. A light colored, but dense bodied tile will usually provide a reasonably stain-resistant installation.

There is a test method to evaluate the stain resistance of ceramic tiles. This test is a simple procedure in which ketchup and other food products are applied to the surface of the tile and evidence of staining is observed. The manufacturer's recommendations for use is also valuable in determining the stain resistance and maintenance requirements of a particular tile.

Penetrating sealers can be applied to unglazed tiles to increase their cleanability and stain resistance. These products are subsurface sealers that fill the microscopic pores in tile. They work most effectively on the more porous types of tile that are classified as semivitreous or nonvitreous. Usually, the appearance of the tile is not altered. Light-colored unglazed tiles often benefit from the application of sealers, because the tiles will become noticeably easier to clean.

Topical sealers, or surface coatings, are also available for use on unglazed tile. These products can increase stain resistance but can become dull and scratched with prolonged wear. An increase in maintenance results, since topical sealers must be periodically stripped and reapplied to eliminate the dulled appearance.

Finally, when researching the maintenance requirements of tile, remember to consider the impact of grout lines. Grout lines are typical problem spots for tile installations since they are slightly lower than the surface of the tile, retain dirt, and can be susceptible to staining. Small tiles such as mosaics have many grout lines, increasing the difficulty of cleaning. Large pavers such as 8" x 8" and 12" x 12" tiles have fewer grout lines and are usually easier to maintain. Penetrating sealers may be applied to cementitious grout to increase its stain resistance. Latex grouts or epoxy grouts have lower absorption rates and will inherently resist staining. Additionally, grouts in neutral colors are preferable for high-traffic areas since both stains and surface dirt are masked in these earthy colors.

Shading in Tiles

Slight irregularities are inherent in all fired products, including all types of ceramic tile. Even with dust-pressed tiles, slight variations in color, size, and texture occur during firing and are a normal part of the manufacturing process.

These variations in ceramic tile are caused by many factors, including minute temperature differences within the kiln and slight differences in the raw materials. For example, in firing, tiles that are closer to the heat source are affected by the higher temperature, and are slightly different from those in the cooler parts of the kiln. Tiles closer to the heat are also slightly more glossy or intense in color and smaller in size.

To increase the uniformity of the product, tiles are sorted into groups with similar appearance and size. Each group of sorted tiles is called a shade. A shade number is given to each group, so that it can be identified and matched with other tiles of the same shade. Usually, this number is marked on each box of tile following the color name and number. Other manufacturers simply use the date of manufacture as identification of the shade.

Having knowledge of shading in ceramic tile is especially important for the do-it-yourselfer. Disappointments can arise when the purchaser is unaware of shades. This problem usually occurs when additional tile is purchased after the first order. If the purchaser orders only a tile name and number and not a shade number, he or she will inevitably get the wrong shade. Not knowing the situation, the purchaser installs the tile, and only after installation is the problem discovered: one tile doesn't exactly match the tile next to it—an undesirable effect.

Additionally, do-it-yourselfers should know that it is important to blend tile from several cartons before installation. Even though the shade numbers match, blending the tile should add uniformity to the installation. You should also check all tiles for defects before installation, since most manufacturer's warranties are void after the tile is installed.

The matching of shade numbers is also necessary when working with two or more different colors of a particular manufacturer's line of tile. The matching shade numbers will insure that the actual (not nominal) tile size of each color is identical, allowing them to fit together without variation in the width of the grout line. This allows more than one color of a particular manufacturer's line of tile to be used together in a pattern.

Chapter *2*

Design Elements

*T*he desire to create order and beauty is a universal human characteristic. It is present in works of art, architecture, graphic design, crafts, and interior design. Likewise, it is present in the planning, production, and creative use of ceramic tile.

This act of creating order and beauty is known as design. It is an active process that seeks to organize parts into a coherent and satisfying whole. Nikolas Pevsner described design as "an aesthetic activity, directed to particular everyday purposes." It is a process that considers both visual and functional viewpoints and results in something original and new. The best designs are those that fulfill their purpose by being both visually and functionally satisfying.

At its most basic level, design is made up of constituent principles or elements. These elements exist in all acts of design, whether in painting, sculpture, or interior design. Elements of design can be thought of as the basic building blocks for creating a design. They include line, space, form, color, texture, pattern, size, and shape. The character of the design, whether good or bad, depends upon the combination of these elements. Successful manipulation of these design elements creates order and beauty.

Ceramic tile, as with all created objects, is subject to the elements of design. Manipulation of the color, size, shape, pattern, and texture alters the appearance of the tile and provides the myriad of choices available today. From multicolored decorative tiles to rustic, brick-red quarry tiles, the design possibilities are seemingly endless. Likewise, the decorative and architectural effects of tile demonstrate a wide range of design possibilities. Tiles can alter the feeling of spaciousness in a room or they can be used to disguise awkward angles or forms. They may be vividly colored and patterned to create a decorative focal point, or they may be muted, monochromatic tiles used to produce unifying or enlarging effects. Let's explore just a few of the possibilities that ceramic tile offers through manipulation of the elements of design.

Color

Color is the most powerful of the design elements and the most obvious characteristic of ceramic tile. The color of a tile can evoke strong emotional and psychological responses based on culture and personal taste. These responses must be considered along with the simple visual effect of a color or combination of colors of tile.

The enormous popularity of ceramic tile is probably due to their beautiful use of color more than any other visual characteristic. Tiles are made in virtually every color imaginable—from brilliant reds, vibrant yellows, and

▲ 47 The spirited color scheme in this powder room is derived from seven colors of glazed wall tiles set in a riotous, random pattern.

▶ 48 Blue and white is the most popular color combination for ceramic tile. Here, hand-painted delft blue and white tiles surround the tub in this romantic ladies bath. A custom-sculpted ceramic-framed mirror coordinates with the tiles and adds depth to the small space.

deep royal blues to pale greens and subtle peach tones. Oranges, pinks, purples, whites, and blacks are also commonly available. Some manufacturers provide tile that is color-coordinated with other tiles in order to simplify the selection process. Other manufacturers provide tile colors that match other materials such as plastic laminate, wallpaper, and plumbing fixtures.

The most traditional tile colors are blue and white. The Chinese first used blue and white on their intricate pottery designs, but they were later popularized for ceramic tile in 16th-century Delft, Holland. The Spanish and Portuguese varied the blue-and-white designs by adding gold or yellow accents to their decorative tiles. Blue and white, and blue, white, and gold decorative tiles continue in popularity today and are manufactured in sever-

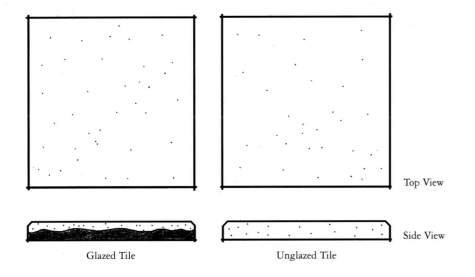

Top View

Side View

Glazed Tile   Unglazed Tile

◄ 49 Glazed tiles and unglazed tiles can sometimes be difficult to differentiate when viewed from the top. Examination of the side and back of the tile will expose the existence of a glaze, since the surface coloration will not continue through the body of the tile. In contrast, the surface coloration of unglazed tiles will continue through the body. Hence, the term "through body" is often used to describe unglazed tiles.

al countries including Italy, Spain, Mexico, and the United States. Kitchens, baths, and fireplace surrounds are common locations for use of these decorative tiles. Sometimes, antique blue and white tiles can be found in auctions or antique stores and used as accents in a field of new, monochromatic, white tiles.

Beyond the traditional colors, ceramic tiles are manufactured in an enormous variety of colors to meet the demands of almost any decorating requirement. The difficulty lies not in finding a range of options, but in limiting the choices and selecting a color scheme that is appropriate. Because tile manufacturers regularly adjust their color selections to match fashion trends, current color schemes are easily created. Many manufacturers employ designers and color forecasters to assist them in selecting current colors.

If none of the standard colors are appropriate, custom colors can be made by many manufacturers. This option usually depends on the square footage that the manufacturer must make per production run, and the quantity you are requesting. The smaller tile manufacturers are often more likely to make small quantities of special colors, since their run quantity is smaller. Often, additional charges are incurred to make a color match, and additional time is also required for manufacturing. Any small paint chip or fabric sample will work to obtain a color match.

Glazed tiles offer the most intense and wide-ranging color palette of all types of ceramic tile. While they are beautiful, you should remember that intensely colored glazed tiles are sometimes soft and don't wear as well as the lighter and more muted glazed colors. This functional concern may affect your choice of colors on areas such as floors and kitchen countertops. Often,

▲ 50 The Spanish often incorporate blue, white, and gold in their tile designs. This tile is a reproduction of Catalan tiles produced in Spain during the 17th century.

▶ 51 This palette of glazed tiles demonstrates the intensity and range of color available in this type of ceramic tile.

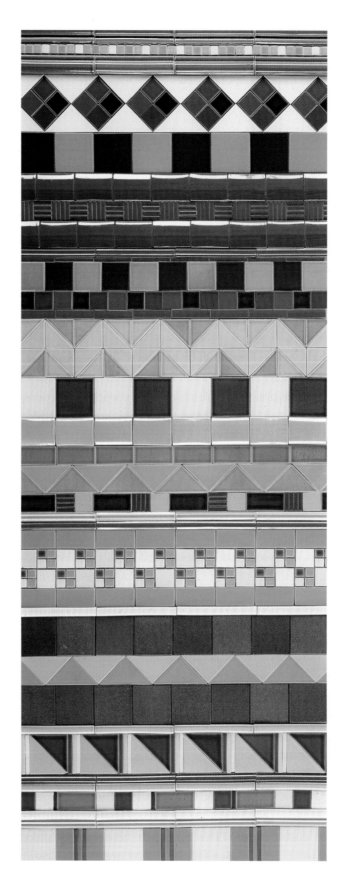

▲ 52 Unglazed porcelain paver tiles have a wide-ranging but more subtle color palette than glazed tiles.

when a design scheme requires intense tile colors, they must be used on walls instead of floors. Remember to check with the manufacturer for their recommendations for use, and review test results if necessary.

Unglazed tiles are usually manufactured in a more muted color palette, but recent advances in manufacturing have produced some brighter hues. Sometimes glazed and unglazed tiles can be combined to create an original decorative effect.

Using White

Regardless of trends in fashion, white has always been the most popular and versatile color of ceramic tile. Tile manufacturers produce a wide variety of white tiles in numerous shades, sizes, shapes, textures, and styles. From smooth, glossy textures to roughened, handmade looks, white tiles are appropriate in all kinds of settings. Victorian tilemakers preferred brick-shaped white tiles or delicate white relief designs that are still manufactured today. Many modern, high-tech kitchens also employ white tiles in glossy, highly uniform $4^{1}/_{4}$" x $4^{1}/_{4}$" or 6" x 6" squares.

▲ 53 These luminous glazed floor tiles reflect the light and visually enlarge the space.

White tiles work especially well in small spaces, since white enlarges the feel of a space by making the walls appear to recede. Installation of white tile on both the floors and walls emphasizes this enlarging effect, since the tile has a monolithic appearance. Decorative tiles or borders may be used to add a touch of interest or color without adversely affecting the enlarging effect. Dark spaces also benefit from the use of white, since white tiles reflect light and serve to brighten dark, windowless rooms. Small, dark powder rooms are excellent candidates for the use of white tiles.

▲ 54 White, tulip relief tiles and moldings add subtle visual interest to walls.

The versatility of white tile is especially evident when it is combined with other colors. Often a field of white tile is interspersed with accents of blue, green, red, or yellow. Depending on the accent color, the effect can be calming, exciting, or playful. Black accents in a white field convey a classic look that is equally suitable for a sophisticated entry hall, living room, kitchen, or bath.

Warm Tones/Dark Colors

Warm tones are some of the most gentle and romantic colors for ceramic tile. Peach, salmon, mauve, beige, honey, and rose make excellent decorating colors because they are subtle and easy on the eye. Glazed wall tiles are available in many warm colors, and the effect is enhanced by the glowing semi-gloss or high-gloss glaze. Warm-colored, glazed wall tiles also work well when combined with other monochromatic warm colors or with decorative tiles in delicate floral or pastoral scenes. An old-world elegance can easily be created with warm colors, since they work well with many decorative antique tiles and with golden or dark-wood antique furnishings. In contrast, ultra-contemporary Memphis style interiors also work well when several solid-colored, warm-toned tiles are combined in geometric patterns. The effect can be stimulating and adventurous.

Warm-colored tiles are also popular for their positive effect on the appearance of skin tones. This benefit is especially evident when warm-col-

▶ 55 A warm, intimate atmosphere is created using dark woods and the rich, brown tones of these Victorian florals and monochromatic glazed wall tiles.

▲ 56 This striking floral mural derives its coloration from vibrantly colored glazes that were hand-painted and fired onto the surface of the tile.

ored, glazed wall tiles are used in mirrored spaces such as bathrooms and powder rooms. The psychological response to the warm color is obvious, since people feel good about themselves in these spaces.

The darker warm tones, such as brown, terra cotta, and brick-red make rooms feel warm and intimate. This color scheme is appropriate for larger spaces that might otherwise seem cold and austere. Large bathrooms, living-room floors, and large country kitchens are excellent choices for brown or rust colored quarry tile or terra cotta tile. Brown, cream, or gold glazed wall tiles and decorative tiles coordinate and complete the design. The effect is warm, earthy, and intimate.

Creating Drama

Drama may be created in a room through the use of high-intensity colors of ceramic tile. Colors such as bright red, black, gold, and midnight blue attract attention and create a focal point for the eye to rest on. These color schemes work best in glazed tiles, since the glazed tiles are more intensely colored than their muted, unglazed counterparts. Often, these intense col-

◄ 57 The subtle variegated coloring of these quarry tiles adds an understated elegance to this dining room floor.

ors are soft-glazed, so that they are limited to wall use. Kitchen backsplashes, stove surrounds, fireplaces, and fountains are often natural focal points that are excellent locations for intensely colored ceramic tiles.

High-contrast color schemes also create drama in a space. The colors need not be intense, since it is the contrast between colors that attracts attention. Traditional combinations, such as blue and yellow or peach and green, provide an exciting contrast in color. The dark tile appears darker because of its placement next to the light tile. Likewise, the light tile seems brighter because the contrast in colors is accentuated. Other more unusual combinations, such as purple and red, are both exhilarating and a bit unsettling. These unusual color combinations should be reserved for spaces in which high drama or surprise is the desired effect.

The most enduring high-contrast color scheme is undeniably black and white. This classic combination of tiles is not only dramatic, but sophisticated and timeless. Many residential bathrooms of the 1920s, 1930s, and 1940s were tiled in combinations of black and white. It is not surprising that these bathrooms are as dramatic and fashionable today as the day they were built.

Subtle Contrasts

Subtle contrasts in the color of ceramic tiles are interesting, yet relaxing and visually undemanding. They are made of combinations of colors with similar hues, values, and intensities. White and beige, gold and brown, and gray and pink are typical combinations.

Subtle contrasts in color are favored by many, because such contrasts tend to outlive fashion trends. The permanency of tile installations lends itself to the use of subtle colors, since you may want to live with your selection for years to come. Subtle color combinations blend into the background and allow other objects in the room to dominate and capture the attention. The floors of living rooms and bedrooms are good locations for these tiles, since they easily take a back seat to other architectural elements or furnishings. These subtle color schemes are also preferred when the floors of an entire house are finished with ceramic tile. This method provides continuity without being monotonous.

Faience tiles are another way to provide subtle color contrast in installations of ceramic tile. These tiles have slight color variations within each tile and between tiles. This variation provides interest and variety without being overwhelming. Other types of tile, such as certain quarry tiles, also have inherent contrast known as range and flash. Range refers to the subtle mix of colors that are present within a particular color of tile and from tile to tile. Flash refers to a splash of slightly contrasting color that is fired into the base color tile. Red, brown, and gray quarry tiles are sometimes available with range and flash.

▲ 58 This bold black and white tiled floor acts to unify the space and clearly demarcate the patio from the garden beyond. Black and white furnishings and drapes mimic the floor, further emphasizing the effect.

Pattern

The modularity of ceramic tile is ideally suited to the use of pattern. Various types of tile can be fitted together in an infinite variety of unique patterns. It is a method of decoration or ornamentation that is inherently repetitive. A motif used over and over transforms a plain, monochromatic tile installation into a eye-catching surface alive with design. Floors, walls, countertops, stove surrounds, backsplashes, fountains, and pools are all excellent locations for ceramic tile patterns.

Ceramic tile patterns are made by manipulating the size, shape, color, and texture of tile. Several basic methods are used to create patterns, and each method has a different effect on an interior design scheme. Some methods are particularly well suited to providing a visual focal point. Others are more subtle and act to unify the spatial composition or create a mood. It is even possible to use two or more methods in a single design. Several common methods of patterning are listed below:

1. Combine different color tiles of the same size, shape, and texture.

2. Combine different sizes or shapes of tile that have the same color and texture.

3. Combine different textures or finishes of tile that have the same color.

4. Use decorative tiles either alone or combined with plain, monochromatic tiles.

5. Use decorative tiles in a mural design.

Patterns of ceramic tile have been in use for thousands of years. Ancient Egyptian, Greek, and Islamic artisans made wide use of patterns using nature or geometry as inspiration for their designs. Often, patterned or decorative tiles were used as borders surrounding an area of color-coordinated monochromatic tiles. This arrangement prevented the patterns from overwhelming the space and provided a balanced appearance. Adaptations of

▶ 59 The Greek key is still a favorite motif for the border of a mosaic floor.

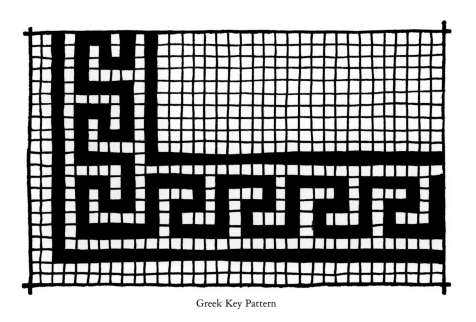

Greek Key Pattern

ancient patterns are commonly available in new ceramic tiles. The Greek key design, stylized water motifs, and curving floral designs are examples of popular patterns that are adapted from ancient designs.

The possibilities for original patterns of ceramic tiles are limitless and are one of the best ways to personalize a home. The unique personality and aesthetic preferences of the homeowner can be creatively expressed in completely new, original combinations of color, size, shape, and texture. Dignified, subtle patterns and bold avant-garde designs are equally possible, given the immense palette of tiles from which you can work. Even traditional designs, such as the checkerboard, can be recreated in unusual or outlandish colors. The checkerboard pattern can also be revamped by using glossy and matte textures of the same color tile.

The use of symbolism, whether cultural or private, is a favorite method for pattern designs. In kitchens, fruit and vegetable motifs remind us of summer and harvests or the owner's love of gardening. In contrast, geometric patterns are symbolic of the kitchen as a functional and efficient work place. Many high-tech kitchens use this symbolism as expressed in sparingly placed squares of color that march along a white tiled backsplash.

Simple Patterns

The long life span of ceramic tile installations suggests that the patterns used should be equally timeless. Simple patterns are among the most enduring of designs, since they are elegant and easy on the eye. They catch your attention without assaulting the senses and provide just enough interest to prevent boredom. Simple patterns are also long-wearing, since they are adaptable to inevitable changes in the room's furnishings, paint colors, and drapes. An elegant entry-hall floor pattern of glossy black squares interspersed throughout a field of cool gray tiles is an example. It works equally well with ornate antiques and pastel fabrics or sleek, chrome furniture and primary colors. You won't need to retile in order to redecorate.

The simplest type of patterning is to use a combination of different sizes or shapes of tile that have the same color and texture. This method works well on floors using porcelain pavers, quarry tiles, terra cotta tiles, or Mexican paver tiles. Often, 8" x 8" and 4" x 4" square tiles are combined with 4" x 8" rectangular tiles, in the same color. Or large hexagonal tiles are fitted together with small, interlocking squares that match in color and texture. This method enlarges and adds continuity to a small home, since the pattern is subtle, and a single floor color is continuous throughout.

White decorative tiles with a delicate swirled corner motif are a well-loved, simple pattern. This classic design works well when used alone or

The simple patterning of this black and white bath creates a time-less elegance that will never go out of style.

with coordinated decorative tiles for a more striking effect. It has an old-world quality that works well in traditional homes and with dark-wood antiques. Other popular patterns include tailored, pin-striped tiles, embossed floral designs, and lacy, monochromatic relief tiles.

Bold Statements

Interiors can be boring without the well-placed use of bold or striking patterns. Bold patterns of ceramic tile are energizing, surprising, and sometimes even unsettling. They often serve to highlight or isolate an important architectural element. Striking patterns can enhance a stove, frame a window, or dramatize an entrance. The patterns may be lavish, elaborate, ornate, forceful, or daring. Because of their wide variety, they are suitable in all types of residences, from the traditional home to the avant-garde apartment. In traditional homes, the fireplace and kitchen are typical locations for lavish or ornate ceramic tiles. Daring and forceful tile patterns are likely to be used anywhere and everywhere in avant-garde residential designs.

▶ 62 Traditional hand-painted tiles are often available in precoordinated designs featuring florals, blanks, and wave borders. The corner motifs tie the composition since they are repeated on every tile.

Murals and decorative tiles are the traditional ways to make a bold statement in ceramic tile. Though they are immediate attention getters, they are rarely overpowering. Both murals and decorative tiles add a rich, custom look to tile installations. Typical themes include florals, fruits and vegetables, animals, and geometric designs. The choice of colors and placement of the design affects the intensity of impact on the space.

Combining different colors and different sizes and shapes of tile in a single design is an especially striking use of pattern. Squares, rectangles, hexagons, and octagons in several sizes and in multiple colors can be combined to create a limitless variety of effects. The result could be whimsical, ironic, dramatic, cheery, lively, refreshing, or stimulating—but rarely monotonous.

▲ 63 This extravagant trompe l'oeil ceramic mural creates the illusion of classical architectural elements.

Combining Patterns

Borders and moldings are the easiest way to combine patterns of ceramic tile. Since the tile manufacturers have already prematched pleasing colors and patterns, the effect is always satisfying. You only have to decide the patterns you prefer that will best suit the interior of your home. Usually, monochromatic field tiles are combined with color-coordinated patterned borders in a myriad of designs. Another option is to combine two distinct patterns such as checks with florals, or pin stripes with scrolls. Stripes, geometrics, dots, ribbons, ropes, garlands, zigzags, vines, and trellises all work well on borders and moldings.

Creating Illusions

Patterns can be used to create illusions in interiors. They have the power to make rooms feel larger or more intimate, or emphasize the horizontal or vertical. A dark, striking pattern on a light background can even have a three-dimensional effect. Patterns are used to accentuate certain architectural elements and minimize others. A plain window seat is given preeminence in a room by accenting it with lively patterns reminiscent of tribal African designs. Or a kitchen stove becomes the heart of the home when awash in the color and pattern of decorative tiles in fruit, vegetable, and floral designs.

A different kind of illusion is used to make new homes feel old. Antique tiles, with scenes of birds, florals, animals, and landscapes are able to imbue newly constructed homes with an historic quality. Antique blue delftware remains a popular choice for facing traditional fireplaces, as it adds a sense of history and romance to the room. New tiles of time-honored designs are also available and will have a similar effect.

Illusions are a great way to add whimsy and surprise to tile installations. A family room floor of solid and patterned ceramic mosaics can appear as a colorful area rug placed appropriately between the sofa and hearth. Ceramic mosaics adapt beautifully to traditional kilim rug designs in bold, multi-colored, geometric patterns. More traditional trompe l'oeil effects can be created in ceramic murals. Rich moldings, columns, friezes, and other interesting architectural elements can be imitated through custom trompe l'oeil mural designs.

Size and Shape

Manipulation of size and shape adds another intriguing dimension to the decorative potential of ceramic tile. Size and shape are important characteristics to consider, since they further establish the overall design scheme. The style and mood of a space is significantly altered by the simple manipulation of size and shape. For example, the effect of a simple black and white checkerboard pattern in 1" x 1" ceramic mosaics is strikingly different from that same checkerboard in 12" x 12" porcelain pavers. The large checkerboard is dramatic, while the small version is charming or quaint. Likewise, a terra cotta floor of plain square tiles has a more rigid and static appearance than one of angular hexagons and octagons or curving ogee designs.

Changes in size and shape are used to accentuate an element or add needed detail. These changes can be accomplished with or without changes in color and texture. Many manufacturers offer tiles in coordinated sizes and shapes that encourage creative designs. In glazed wall tiles, square 6" x 6" tiles module with 3" x 3" and $4^{1}/_{4}$" x $4^{1}/_{4}$" tiles that are turned on the diagonal. Porcelain pavers are also modular in 12" x 12", 8" x 8", 6" x 6", 4" x 4", and 4" x 8" tiles. Squares, rectangles, hexagons, octagons, diamonds, triangles, ogee shapes, and occasionally even circles are available from modern tile manufacturers, although squares are the most traditional shape.

▲ 64 Broken tile shards are used to create an irregular pattern on this distinctive kitchen countertop. The shards are inlaid in a field of 6" x 6" tiles cut along diagonal lines.

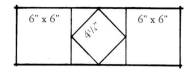

▲ 65 It's easy to create patterns using standard sizes of glazed wall tiles. Turn a typical 4¼" x 4¼" tile on the diagonal and a diamond shape results. Then frame the diamond with standard 6" x 6" tiles.

Interior design is an ambiguous art, so there are no firm rules to guide the selection of size and shape of tile. It is not always true that small rooms require small tiles and large rooms need large tiles. There are far too many factors involved to make that assumption, factors such as angles and obstructions, function, style, mood, continuity, directional lines, rhythm, proportion, and balance. Instead, it is probably more true that cluttered, irregular spaces—whether large or small—benefit from larger tiles. This is true because there are fewer grout lines to crowd and visually divide the space. Similarly, countertops also benefit from larger tiles, since the grout lines can be susceptible to stains.

From the contractor's viewpoint, it is better not to use the same size tile on both walls and floors. Designs of this type usually require that the floor and wall tiles line up, which is next to impossible given the imperfections of construction. Rooms are rarely perfectly square due to inaccuracies in rough framing or settling of the foundation. The most practical choice is to have one size of tile on the floor and a different size on the wall. However, the placement of the floor tile on the diagonal provides another solution, since this also eliminates the need for wall and floor tile alignment.

Many manufacturers produce tile intended to align on walls and floors, since this is a popular design theme. Modern and minimalist designs often require this monolithic, uncluttered appearance. If this scheme is utilized, it can be worked out to ensure the tile will align on at least one wall, despite imperfections in construction. This is done by selecting one wall for alignment and starting the tile layout on that wall. This wall, known as the feature wall, should be the most prominent wall in the room. Other, less visually important walls may be unaligned, since the unaligned tile is less noticeable there.

Small Options

Ceramic mosaics are, by definition, the smallest of all tiles. Typical sizes include 1" x 1", 1" x 2", 2" x 2", and 1" hexagons. They are also the most versatile, due to the large number of sizes, shapes, and colors. Squares, rectangles, hexagons, and circles are commonly available.

Small tiles permit, even encourage, the use of details that are not possible in larger tiles. Complex border and field patterns and intricate murals, logos, and lettering are all possible. A common use of mosaic lettering is for depth markers at the waterline of pools. Linear and geometric designs are easily created, but curvalinear designs can also be achieved using 1" squares or 1" hexagons and half-hexagon shapes. Even flowing floral designs can be created, though the look is abstract.

▲ 66 This quaint bath features 2" x 2" ceramic mosaics and liners. The contrasting border frames the room and draws attention to the perimeter shelf.

Small tiles are often associated with quaint or provincial interiors. Dainty checks, stripes, and dots lend themselves to a country kitchen and breakfast nook. The look is both simple and charming. Though less common, bold large-scale patterns are also possible using small tiles. These bold patterns are created by joining several small tiles of the same color into large-scale designs.

With regard to installation, there are several advantages to using small tiles. Curved surfaces are more easily faced, and slight imperfections in the substrate are more easily tolerated using mosaic tiles. Still, imperfections and deflection of the substrate should be corrected, not ignored. Installation is also simple since these small tiles are mounted on sheets.

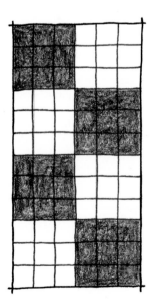

▲ 67 Ceramic mosaics can be used to create large-scale patterns.

Larger Statements

The beauty of large tiles lies in their ability to provide a feeling of strength
and permanence to a room. They have a solid, substantial quality, unlike
their smaller counterparts. This look is especially attractive when used on
floors, but some walls also benefit from this appearance. Porcelain pavers,
glazed pavers, quarry tiles, and terra cotta tiles are all available in large sizes.
Some of these tiles can be as large as 48" x 48", although this is rare.

Large tiles also work well in combination with other elements in a room.
They are large enough to create a pleasing contrast with patterned wallpaper, fabrics, accessories, area rugs, and small ceramic tiles. Large tiles offset
the busyness of these elements and provide a unifying and calming effect.
An additional benefit is that design schemes are easily created with large
tiles, since patterning is usually not complex.

A favorite use of large tiles is to create a contrasting or patterned border
at the perimeter of the floor. This scheme works well in large rooms, since

it defines the space and makes the room feel smaller and more intimate. In contrast, monolithic, enlarging looks can be created by using large, solid-colored tiles with matching grout. For example, a cluttered guest bath seems larger with light colored 6" x 6" wall and floor tiles installed with matching grout. For a different effect, a highly contrasting grout color can be used to emphasize the grid and size of the tiles. This effect can be both striking and surprising, since it is not often used.

Rectangular Shapes

Squares and rectangles are the most traditional shapes for ceramic tile. They work well in many spaces, since most homes are composed of rectangles. Doors, windows, furniture, fireplaces, cabinetry, walls, and the overall shape of floors are usually rectangular. Square and rectangular tiles fit neatly into these simple, 90° spaces.

Squares are a static shape suggesting stability, calm, and order. They blend into the architecture and don't call attention to themselves. A more dynamic use of square tiles can be created by placing them on the diagonal. On floors, this interesting approach will make spaces seem larger and can be used to create angular, directional lines.

Rectangles are also a stable shape. When placed horizontally on walls, rectangular tiles are restful and relaxing, having the appearance of bricks that are stacked on each other. Vertical rectangles are a bit more lively, especially if they are long and thin. On walls, vertically placed rectangles set end on end work well in high-tech decorative schemes. A clean, crisp, machine-like effect is produced through use of this simple geometry.

Patterns of rectangular tiles provide another variation on this theme. Traditional brick patterns are especially popular, including diagonal herringbone, basketweave, and running bond. The herringbone and basketweave patterns work best on floors, since these patterns are too busy to be used on most walls.

Angular Shapes

Angular shapes have a dynamic and exciting quality. They suggest movement, energy and activity. Because the eye is accustomed to rectangular shapes with 90° angles, angular tiles are perceived as different and unusual. Hexagons, octagons, pentagons, diamonds, and triangles are examples of angular tiles, and they are produced in a range of sizes. Depending on the type of tile, sizes can range from approximately 1" to 12". Ceramic mosaics, quarry tiles, glazed paver tiles, and terra cotta tiles are commonly available in angular shapes.

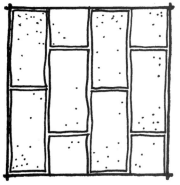

Running Bond

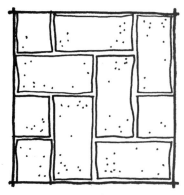

Herringbone

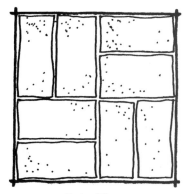

Basket Weave

▲ 69 Traditional brick patterns can be created by using 4" x 8" quarry or paver tiles. The same look is achieved, but without the added weight and thickness of brick.

▶ 70 The use of standard, square tiles need not be repetitious and dull. This dramatic bath features square tiles that compose an eye-catching wall motif.

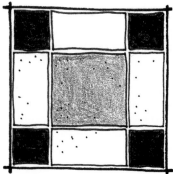

▲ 71 Many large scale tiles are modular, allowing them to be combined with other sizes of tile. This drawing demonstrates a pattern using modular 8" x 8", 4" x 8", and 4" x 4" tiles.

The beauty of angular tiles lies in their ability to fit together like pieces of a puzzle. The effect is sophisticated and classic. Many variations are possible, since the five basic angular shapes can be elongated or shortened to create different looks. Most angular tiles, such as hexagons, diamonds, and triangles, can be used alone without the need for other shapes to complete the pattern. In contrast, octagons and pentagons require a square tile to complete the puzzle design. Often, the square tile is small and of a contrasting color. Terra cotta octagons and cobalt blue accent squares are a popular and timeless option.

Angular tiles are rarely used on walls, except as accents. This is because angular tiles seem visually unstable when installed vertically. Instead, angular tiles are used widely in residential flooring applications.

Curved Shapes

Curved tile shapes suggest movement and fluidity. They add a graceful rhythm to ceramic tile designs. Sometimes these tiles are intricate and detailed and fit together with other curved shapes or circles. The effect is both soothing and exotic. Other curved designs, such as mosaic circles, are used only with other circles. Circles, ogee, and Moorish shapes are examples of curved tiles.

Except for mosaic circles, curved shapes are commonly produced only in terra cotta. Solid-colored terra cotta tiles lend themselves beautifully to these gentle swirling patterns. Often, these tiles are used to add a Mediterranean feeling to rooms. Patios, terraces, sunrooms, and pool decks are favorite locations for these exotic shapes.

▲ 72 This elaborate pinwheel border and black cat demonstrate hand-cut angular tiles.

◄ 73 Movement is suggested in the flowing curves of this harlequin-motif tabletop.

▲ 74 The use of both smooth and hammered-texture tiles adds subtle interest to this Arts-and-Crafts–style fireplace. Hand-painted Art Nouveau tree tiles provide additional impact.

Texture

Texture, or the surface quality of a tile, enhances the other elements of design: color, pattern, size, and shape. Texture can make colors appear brighter or more muted, patterns and sizes can enlarge or recede, and the shape can be emphasized or made less prominent. Texture also affects how the tile looks when light strikes it, and how it feels to the touch. It can even make a tile seem newly made or antique. An enormous range of decorative effects are possible by simply altering the texture of ceramic tiles.

The use of texture has contributed to the centuries-old popularity of ceramic tile. Texture adds beauty, character, and a feeling of quality. Other smooth-finish materials—such as plastic laminates, sheet vinyl, and resilient flooring—seem, by comparison, to be lifeless, characterless, and cheap. They lack the enduring spirit that texture can imbue. Similarly, texture also contributes to the feeling of permanency in ceramic tiles. As with time-roughened, antique furniture, textured ceramic tiles delight the senses with subtle, modulating patterns of light and dark. Even scratches and small chips add to their character, giving tiles a pleasing, antique look.

Textures are particularly important in interior design as they add both physical and emotional comfort to our surroundings. Variations in texture add interest and variety to homes, since the changes catch the eye and delight the hand. A minimalist living room with all smooth textures can be cold, uninviting, and visually uninteresting. Its machinelike effect could be softened with fabrics, plants, and textured furniture. In contrast, a rustic den with a rich variety of textures on walls, floors, and furniture can be pleasing and comfortable. It is neither boring nor overpowering, since the eye and hand experience changing sensations.

Ceramic tiles are available in two basic types of textures: tactile and visual. Tactile textures can be felt, since they result from actual changes in plane. The indentations of Victorian relief tiles, glassy smoothness of glazed wall tiles, and gentle undulations of handcrafted Mexican paver tiles are examples of tactile textures. In contrast, visual textures merely give the impression of texture through variations in light and dark. Many glazed ceramic tiles are visually textured, since they are perfectly smooth to the touch, yet appear to have surface irregularities. Flecks of color, suspended in the glaze, give this appearance of texture. For example, glazed faience tiles have subtle variations in color that give the impression of roughness or depth.

Texture also tells us something about the way tiles are made. Handmade tiles have a noticeably different appearance from machinemade tiles. Handmade tiles have highly valued variety and warmth in their textures.

Machines are unable to capture this effect, since their textures are more uniform and precise. Each machinemade tile is alike, creating a sleek, uncluttered ambience in rooms. This decorative effect is also prized by many.

Texture is also an important factor in the maintenance of ceramic tiles. The shiny surfaces of monochromatic, glazed tiles are impervious and easy to clean, but readily show fingerprints and smudges. Rougher, unglazed tiles, such as porcelain pavers and quarry tiles, call less attention to dirt but can be harder to clean. The best way to decrease maintenance is to use smooth surfaces with flecks of color that add visual texture to a tile.

Smooth and Glossy

Tiles that are characteristically smooth and glossy come in two basic categories: glazed tiles and polished tiles. These tiles are similar in appearance, and are produced by automated machines in modern die presses. Smooth, glossy tiles may be either glazed wall tiles, glazed paver tiles, polished porcelain pavers, or polished porcelain mosaics. They have perfectly flat, uniform shapes and a shiny finish. Glossy glazed tiles are also available in handmade varieties, but they are distinguishable from the machinemade types, since their surface is not smooth and flat.

Smooth, glossy tiles work especially well in minimalist interiors, because they have a crisp, clean appearance. These tiles are also excellent choices to reflect light and enlarge small, dark spaces. Polished porcelain pavers cladding both floor and backsplash lend themselves to the sophisticated ambiance of a small, high-tech kitchen. The look is light, sleek, and efficient. Glazed paver tiles can also be used to create much the same effect, but at less cost.

Bathrooms, kitchens, and entries are excellent locations for smooth, glossy tiles, since these are typically high-maintenance areas. These tiles resist dirt and stains and are easily cleanable. Smooth glossy tiles can be slippery if used on floors, and some glazes are prone to showing scratches. Therefore, the manufacturer's recommendations for use should be carefully observed. In addition, glossy tiles should be avoided in apartments for the elderly, since the tiles' reflection can cause confusion and disorientation.

Honed and Matte

Honed and matte tiles are similar in appearance, but their surface texture is achieved in different ways. Honed tiles are unglazed tiles that have been ground to a smooth, dull finish. The manufacturing technique is the same as with polished tiles, but the grinding time is shortened. Matte finish tiles

▲ 75 The sleek character of this small bath is derived from the use of glossy, glazed wall tiles in iridescent shades of copper and gold.

are glazed tiles with a dull, no-shine surface. Both types are produced in solid and speckled colors.

There are functional advantages to using honed and matte tiles rather than glossy tiles. First, they are less slippery and show minimal scratching. For this reason, many honed and matte tiles are suitable for floors and countertops where glossy tiles are not appropriate. Second, honed and matte tiles are preferred in areas where finger prints and soap scum are likely to build up. This type of dirt is somewhat hidden by these unreflective tile surfaces when installed on countertops and tub surrounds.

▲ 76 These matte glazed paver tiles have a durable surface that is easy to clean and masks both scratches and dirt.

◀ 77 Inspired by Egyptian mythology, the design of this beautiful tile is reminiscent of the large burial pendants worn by ancient Egyptian rulers.

Rustic

Rustic tiles may be either machinemade or handmade. Both types have a somewhat roughened, natural texture that often works best when used on floors. Handmade, rustic tiles are usually irregularly shaped or the surface may be uneven and undulating. Machinemade rustic tiles are dimensionally uniform, but have a rough, textured surface. Rustic tiles, whether machinemade or handmade, are usually unglazed and earth-colored in red, orange, brown, tan, and warm gray. Quarry tiles, terra cotta tiles, and handmade glazed wall tiles are examples of rustic tiles.

Mexican floor tiles are favorites among rustic tiles. They have an earthy, roughened appearance that is a pleasing backdrop for many interiors. Some varieties are available with a randomly placed animal imprint on the surface. This occurs when a dog or chicken happens to stray across the surface as the tiles were drying in the sun. Mexican floor tiles work especially well in southwest-flavored schemes when combined with white stucco walls, primitive furniture, and textured fabrics. Still, these adaptable tiles work equally well in such diverse decorating schemes as country, postmodern, or Memphis.

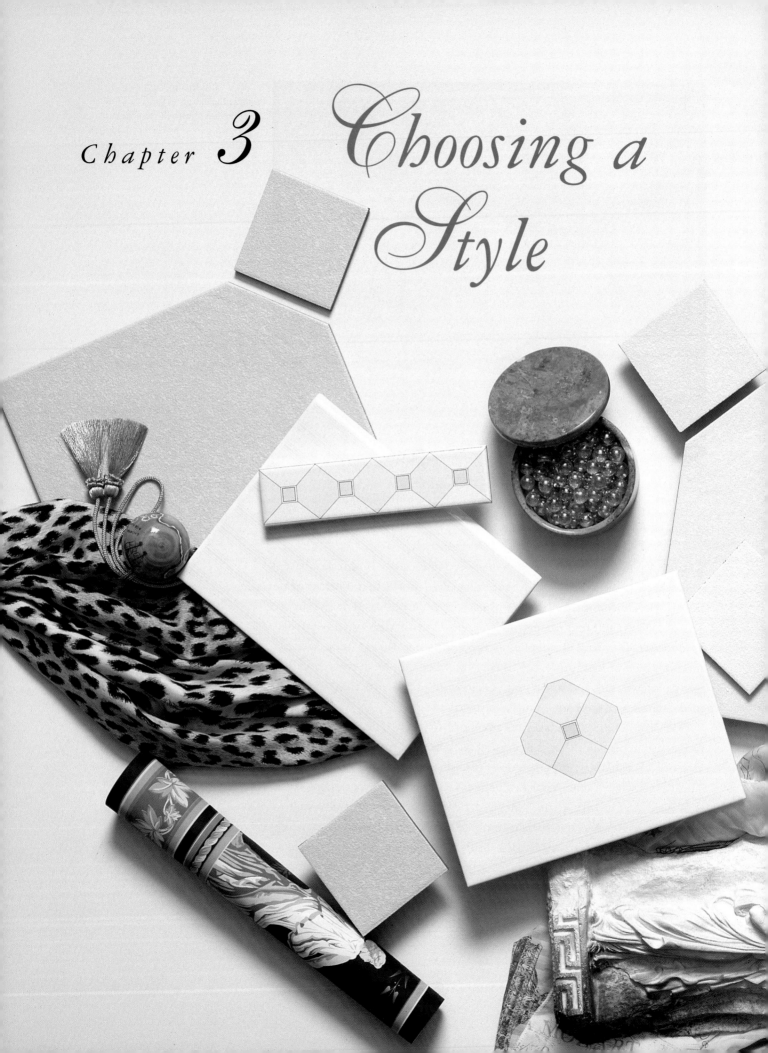

Chapter **3** *Choosing a Style*

$\mathcal{I}$n the last chapter, we learned of the universal human desire to create order. This desire is especially evident in the need to organize, beautify, and personalize the living space or home. The selection of interior finishes and the choice and placement of furniture provide an important means to create order. Personal expression and the owner's unique aesthetic preferences are also reflected in these choices. The resulting arrangement is so important to the human psyche that it can affect one's mood and outlook.

In the context of interior design, the word *style* is used to refer to the distinctive flair of a home. This style or flair is the result of the owner's personal expression, aesthetic preferences, and values. The style of a home makes a visual statement about the owner's values and tells people what the owner wants to project.

A second definition of the word style refers to the characteristic furnishings, architecture, and designs of a particular culture at a given period in history. Eighteenth century English and French furnishings are examples of elegant period styles that remain popular today. Sometimes, period styles are used literally and entire rooms may be decorated with period furnishings, draperies, and finishes. More often, the style or distinctive flair of a home draws on the spirit of a period style. The style is merely an adaptation of forms from other cultures, allowing the design to retain a current outlook. It is extremely rare to find a home that does not exhibit at least some influence of a period style.

Ceramic tile allows for a wide range of personal expression because of its versatility. Different colors, sizes, shapes, patterns, and textures of tile have different effects on the interior design of a home and can be adapted to many diverse styles and design schemes. Tile can be used as a backdrop to furnishings and fabrics or serve as a visual focal point. It can disguise awkward architectural elements and adapt to both traditional and contemporary designs. Even traditional period styles can be replicated using antique tiles or new tiles of time-honored designs.

Choosing a style for your ceramic tile project is a very personal decision with no hard and fast rules to guide your selection. The beauty of designing with ceramic tile is in its adaptability to your personal style.

Tile as the Backdrop

A popular design solution is to use ceramic tile as the backdrop to other interior finishes and elements. The tile becomes an integral part of the architecture of the home, like the walls, ceiling, doors, and windows. This use of tile also enhances the feeling of permanency in a room, since the tile does not feel decorative or applied.

▲ 78 Ceramic tile is an integral part of the architecture of this elegant room. The marble fireplace, rich wood moldings, and glazed paver tiles all contribute to the sense of quality and permanence in this home.

When tile is used as a backdrop, it takes a subordinate position to other elements in the room. Furnishings, draperies, rugs, accessories, windows, or the fireplace are emphasized and become the dominant feature. In a Victorian bathroom, a claw-foot tub becomes the focus when plain, monochromatic glazed tiles are installed on walls and floors. A balance, pleasing to the eye, is created between the dominant and subordinate elements.

Floors are excellent locations for ceramic tile. When installed throughout several rooms, the background of tile unifies and enlarges the interior design of the home. The tile's homogeneous color and texture are both calming and restful. Area rugs work particularly well when set on the background of a ceramic tile floor. The rug creates a focal point, adds softness and warmth, and defines a separate area within the room. Living rooms, bedrooms, kitchens, dining rooms, bathrooms, and entries are all excellent locations for this combination of floor tile and area rugs.

The functionality of tiles is emphasized when they are unadorned and allowed to blend into the architecture. They make a statement of function that can appear clinical, especially when used on bathroom walls. Plumbing fixtures take on a dominant position emphasizing the hygienic purpose of the room. The function of the kitchen stove, sink, and food preparation areas are also spotlighted when plain white tiles are used in the backsplash. Widely spaced monochromatic relief decorative tiles can be used to soften the somewhat impersonal effect.

There are many different types of tiles that can work as a backdrop in the interior design of a home. Plain, unadorned quarry tiles, glazed wall tiles, paver tiles, and terra cotta tiles can all be used in this manner. Even mosaics can serve as a backdrop, as long as a single color is used—without the addition of pattern. Rustic Mexican floor tiles are perhaps the most popular tile for this design scheme. Often elegant and sophisticated furnishings are used in contrast to the rustic backdrop of these handmade tiles.

Monolithic Looks

Monolithic tile designs have a simple, uncluttered look that works as a natural backdrop to other elements in a room. These designs are usually created using large, matching, monochromatic tiles on both walls and floors. Matching grout color is also used to minimize the appearance of the grout lines. If ornament or accent colors are used in the tilework, a sparse, sleek, minimalist style is created.

These sleek, monolithic tile designs produce a style that emphasizes the sense of space in a room. The room's geometry, spatial intentions, and structure are enhanced, and become the dominant feature. This style was first

▲ 79 A touch of the Orient is apparent in the design of this master bath and meditation room. The minimalist style is created using mosaics with a matching grout color. The contours of the room are emphasized with a contrasting tile border set at chair-rail height.

developed in Germany by the Bauhaus School, where function, utility, and expressions of mass production were encouraged. It later became known as the International Style, since it was deemed the universal expression of modern life. This style continues to have a profound effect on both modern interior design and modern tile design.

Bathrooms are perhaps the best location for monolithic tile designs. Since these rooms are usually small, monolithic tile adds an unbroken continuity and spaciousness. Italian tile manufacturers particularly favor this sophisticated look and produce many large, glazed tiles in sizes and shapes that align on walls and floors. Typically, large glazed rectangular tiles are used on walls, with matching square, glazed tiles on floors. Though smaller tiles have traditionally been the mainstay of U. S. manufacturers, they have also recently begun to produce these larger glazed tiles.

▲ 80 Muted colors impart additional subtlety to these quaint, relief tiles.

Muted Colors

The use of subtle, muted colors is another method used to deemphasize the visual impact of tile installations. The tile is unobtrusive and visually undemanding, since it is unmarked by pattern or intense coloration. Stronger colors can be given to other elements in the room, such as furnishings and window treatments, so that the effect is not dull or bland. Since these elements are less permanent, it is easy to change decorating schemes when an updated look is desired.

Muted colors suggest tranquility and can be used to counteract the busyness of everyday life. They provide a restful background to the clutter of a gourmet kitchen, family bath, or child's playroom. The juxtaposition of brightly colored toys strewn across a whitewashed terra cotta floor is pleasing to the eye. The chaotic jumble of dolls, blocks, and stuffed animals are minimized by the unifying background of tile.

The appearance of wood furnishings and cabinets are also enhanced by soft, muted colors. Since the color of the tile is subdued, the glowing wood finish takes on primary importance and becomes the distinctive feature in the room. Muted pastel tiles work particularly well with kitchen and bathrooms cabinets of red oak, maple, or white pine. This color scheme also works in living rooms, entries, and bedrooms when pale pastel floor tiles are used to complement dark wood antiques.

Tile As the Focus

The striking beauty of ceramic tile lends itself to bold expressions of color, texture, and pattern. This use of tile easily calls attention to itself and creates a visual focal point within a room. Because the tile dominates the space, other elements are naturally less important and should coordinate with the design of the tile. The tile sets the spirit and tone of the room; furnishings, fabrics, and accessories merely enhance the intent of the tile design. If the design of the room is successful, then balance, rhythm, and harmony are achieved between the tile and subordinate elements.

It is important to consider carefully the alternatives in placing tile in order to create a focal point. This is done by noting the unique characteristics of the room and by deciding which elements should be emphasized. Depending on the shape and peculiarities of the room, ceramic tile may be appropriate for enhancing walls, floors, ceilings, windows, or doors. In addition, architectural features such as fireplaces, window seats, and kitchen stoves are natural focal points. Often, these existing features can be highlighted by an accent of brightly colored or patterned tile.

▲ 81 The essence and fecundity of the tropics is captured in this exhilarating mosaic mural. The glass tiles were individually cut and fitted by hand to create this intricate and striking design.

Also, a focal point or accent of ceramic tile can be used to add character to plain, featureless rooms. Often, the rooms of modern homes are bland, utilitarian spaces that lack the beauty of traditional architectural ornament. With the addition of ceramic tile moldings, picture tiles, or murals, these rooms can be imbued with character reminiscent of many older homes. Ceramic tile wainscoting, chair rail and crown moldings, door and window facings, and trompe l'oeil murals can add needed richness and interest.

A focal point of tile can also be used to alter the perception of space. Often, this method is used to disguise an awkward element such as an uncomfortable layout of a room. If the room is too long and narrow, it can be made to appear less confining by the use of a patterned accent wall on one or both ends. Moreover, an uncomfortably large room with a high ceiling can be made smaller and more intimate by emphasizing the ceiling with a dark or boldly patterned ceramic tile ceiling.

There are many different types of tiles that can be used to create a visual focal point in the interior design of a home. Intensely colored glazed wall tiles, mosaics, quarry tiles, paver tiles, moldings, and decorative tiles are just

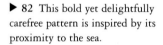

▶ 82 This bold yet delightfully carefree pattern is inspired by its proximity to the sea.

◀ 83 A vibrant, red tile floor and countertop enliven this windowless bathroom that gets little natural light.

a few examples. Each of these tiles can be used as accent colors or to create visually exciting patterns, borders, and murals.

Accent Colors

Accent colors can be used to create eye-catching tile designs that provide a room's visual focal point. These boldly colored tiles excite the senses and evoke a strong response from the viewer. Vivid accent colors create a stimulating environment that largely determines the style, mood, and spirit of the room. The room's fabrics, furnishings, and wall coverings become secondary in importance and must naturally coordinate with the color and style of the tile design Usually, the colors of the tile design are reminiscent of a period style such as Arts and Crafts, Memphis, or Victorian.

Accent colors create drama in a space through the use of strong contrast. The contrast is created by the abrupt transition of one intense color placed against another. This contrast is often used to visually divide a space or to distinguish separate functions within a room. For example, the functions of an open plan living/dining room are distinguished with a contrasting tile color placed beneath the dining room table. This use of color can also work to make the large, undefined space appear smaller, cozier, and more intimate.

Glazed tiles are the best way to employ accent colors. For walls, the palette of shimmering glazed wall tiles is enormous: intense reds, blues, greens, and yellows, as well as black, white, and violet. On floors, glazed paver tiles or glazed mosaics offer the widest range of accent colors. Though more muted, they have a similar effect on a large expanse of floor.

Strong Patterns

Strong patterns of ceramic tile are another method used to determine the style of the room. They are often bold, animated, or whimsical, and they deliberately flaunt their dominant position in the room. Patterned tile has a visual weight that must be counteracted and balanced by patterned upholstery, rugs, or brightly painted cabinets.

Continuity is created when the tile pattern is repeated in a modified version in other design elements. These similar, recurring colors and patterns unify the room without being tiresome or overpowering. For example, in an updated country kitchen, a bold checkerboard pattern of blue and white 8" x 8" glazed floor tile could be repeated in a quaint check fabric used for curtains, chair cushions, or a tablecloth. Or, you could place a band of 1" x 1" check mosaics in the backsplash as an accent in a field of white 6" x 6" glazed wall tile. Altering the scale of the recurring pattern allows the floor pattern to dominate, yet provides a consistent rhythm in the room.

There are many different ways to create strong, eye-catching patterns using ceramic tile. Intricately patterned decorative tiles and borders are perhaps the simplest method, since much of the design work is done for you. You only need to decide on the number and placement of each tile. Ceramic tile murals are another way to create patterns using either stock or customized pictures. Brightly colored fruit and vegetable designs are especial-

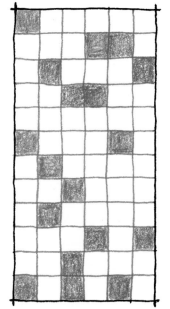

Random Mosaic Pattern

▲ 84 Random mosaic patterns can be factory-mounted onto sheets per your specifications. Simply select two or more colors of tile and identify the percentages of each color. This drawing represents a 2" x 2" random pattern using 75 percent white tiles and 25 percent black.

ly popular for kitchens, while sophisticated florals provide a classic focal point for a tiled fireplace or bar. Lastly, patterns may be created by combining two or more colors of monochromatic tiles. This method provides a limitless range of options for the creative individual to explore.

Moldings

Ceramic moldings are a sophisticated way to add visual interest and create a focal point. The depth, texture, and ornament of these relief moldings attract attention and can add richness to otherwise plain, featureless rooms. Usually, these moldings are glazed and are color coordinated with the manufacturer's palette of glazed wall tiles. They are only appropriate for wall applications, since they project out from the plane of the surrounding tile.

The traditional detail of carved wood moldings can be replicated in ceramic moldings. Ornate crown moldings and chair rails are recreated in durable, water-resistant ceramic in fluted, rope, and ogee designs. Typically, these moldings are manufactured in 6" lengths, and as with tiles, grout is

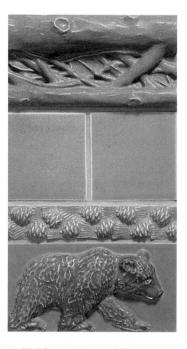

▲ 85 These unique moldings are inspired by nature, depicting tree branches, pine cones, and animals. Because of their dimensional character, their use should be limited to walls and backsplashes.

▲ 86 Ceramic moldings and trim shapes are used to create the rich detail on this extraordinary vanity.

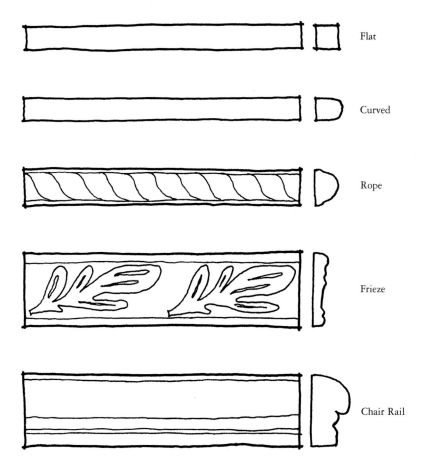

Flat

Curved

Rope

Frieze

Chair Rail

placed between the pieces. They are usually more expensive than their wood counterparts; therefore, their use should be limited to areas where water, grease, and cleanup are a concern. In bathrooms, a popular use of moldings is to frame a mirror to create a custom, built-in look.

Ceramic tile moldings can be used to provide emphasis to existing architectural elements, to alter the scale of a room, or to unify the space. For example, a plain, painted wall becomes a focal point with the addition of ceramic chair rail and crown molding. In addition, the scale of the space can be altered if the crown molding is located several inches below the ceiling. This placement brings down the proportions of a room with high ceilings to a more human scale. These same moldings can also serve to unify the space if they are applied continuously to all walls forming the perimeter of the room.

Ceramic trim tiles can also be used to create a similar effect to moldings. Trim tiles are designed to allow tile installations to round corners, but they can be creatively applied to the flat wall surface to add needed depth and interest. They are less expensive than moldings and can provide a measure of character and richness to walls. Quarter-round beads and curb tile moldings are commonly used for this application.

▲ **88** Tile is the traditional floor material for Italian homes. Here, modular pavers are used to introduce a checkerboard area rug into a field of solid blue tiles. The modern tile design is unexpectedly compatible with the traditional architecture of this historic home.

Traditional Designs

Traditional tile designs draw upon history for their inspiration. They are often some of the most visually interesting tiles, since they are usually highly decorative. Seascapes, florals, fruit, vegetables, animals, birds, fish, lattice designs, arabesques, and garlands are common themes. Traditional tile designs are available in reproductions of historic designs, using time-honored manufacturing techniques. They are also available in new, original designs that are merely inspired by a historic period of tilemaking. Antique English medieval tiles, Art Nouveau floral designs, and Dutch picture tiles can also be purchased for a tile project.

In recent years, the interiors of homes have reflected a renewed interest in historically inspired designs. Period rooms can be recreated following the predominant style of many historic cultures, including Victorian, Regency, Georgian, Arts and Crafts, or Art Nouveau styles. Ceramic tile adapts well to many of these period recreations and adds a feeling of permanency and authenticity to the room. Victorian decorative relief tiles in floral designs remain among the most popular of historic tiles. Delft tiles are also commonly used as accents in recreations of the traditional Early American fireplace.

Traditional tile designs need not be mere imitations of historic tiles. Instead, these designs often serve as a resource for stimulating new ideas for tile designs, allowing for creativity and innovation with unusual color and textural combinations. Likewise, placement and use of the tile need not be traditional. Freshness and originality are created when traditionally inspired tiles are placed in unusual settings, combinations, or arrangements.

Traditional tiles can also be used to soften the cold, impersonal effect of modern appliances. In kitchens and baths, such items as plumbing fixtures, stoves, or microwave ovens can be deemphasized and the spirit of the room enhanced with the shimmering colors of tile. These traditionally inspired tiles blending with the conveniences of modern living add an historic flavor to the room. Often, unpretentious rustic tiles are used to emphasize warmth and the comforts of home. In addition, exhaust hoods, stoves, and sinks are sometimes sheathed in tile to minimize their effect.

There are many types of traditional tiles from which to choose. Decorative picture tiles, relief tiles, murals, and terra cotta tiles convey a sense of tradition and evoke the spirit of the past. Time-honored designs from Spain, Holland, and Italy are often hand-painted by the same families that created them centuries ago. By using these tiles, an authentic, old-world quality can be created in even newly constructed homes.

Country French

This comfortable kitchen and dinette embodies the spirit of French country living without sacrificing the wonders of modern technology. Its old-world quality is derived from the richness of dark woods, traditional detailing, and antique French terra cotta tiles. The soothing earth tones and dark floor contribute to a cozy ambiance even though the spaces are expansive. Floor tiles are set in strips of oak that run diagonally through the rooms. This adds subtle contrast and interest to the design.

The authentic 18th-century terra cotta tiles are used liberally throughout the kitchen. A 12-foot expanse of backsplash and countertop are sheathed in tile, as well as the unusual cornice detail above. Backsplash lighting spotlights the variation in color and texture of these beautiful handmade tiles.

Neo-Gothic

An extravagant neo-Gothic style was chosen for the design of this romantic rooftop conservatory. Rich in embellishments, the Gothic-style tracery, lattices, and stained-glass frieze work well in juxtaposition to the simple patterning of the ceramic tile floor.

Ceramic floor tiles are the perfect choice since they will withstand occasional drips and spills from the many plants in the room. The pale beige tiles are also appropriate since they reflect the light and enlarge the visual dimensions of the space. In addition, the tiles provide needed contrast to the dark furnishings and accessories.

▶ 91

Victorian

This lovely Victorian bath retains all the charm of that gentle era. A reproduction pedestal sink and antique gilt-framed mirror and sconces reinforce the period look. The hand-painted ceramic tile wainscoting visually enlarges the space and adds interest with delicate floral decorative tiles and borders. The ceramic tile is both historically correct and functionally appropriate for this high-humidity environment.

The prominent use of white enlarges the space and prevents the small room from feeling cluttered despite the lavish character of the tile designs. On the floor, coordinated floral tile insets complete the design, tying the composition of walls and floor.

◄ 92

Contemporary Designs

Contemporary tile designs break from the past by rejecting historic period styles. These designs reject the ornament of traditional designs in favor of either monochromatic colors, simple geometric patterns, or bold polychromatic statements. The artist and craftsman are also rejected in favor of machinemade products. Industrialism, science, and mass production are viewed as the perfect expression of the modern world.

Contemporary, machine-age designs were first promoted by the artistic avant-garde of the 1910s, 1920s, and 1930s. These tastemakers based their designs on the political and ideological concepts of the time, which emphasized utility, practicality, and simplicity. The designs of Le Corbusier (1887–1965) and the Bauhaus School in Germany (1919–1933) were at the forefront of this movement. Their designs, whether for cities, public housing, or common household items, were equally imaginative, yet functional, austere, and uniform. This new ideology also rejected individualism. As a result, the Bauhaus ceramics department was eventually closed, since the craft was deemed too individual.

The new materials and methods of the machine age provided an entirely new aesthetic for ceramic tile. Clean lines, smooth surfaces, and perfect uniformity were admired, whereas the imperfect, irregular handmade tile was considered to be obsolete. Mass production also made tile more accessible to the public as its availability increased and price was reduced. Technological advances produced improvements in the quality of tile, as precision of size and shape, harder glazes, and denser bodies were developed.

The colors and patterns of contemporary tile designs also took on a crisp, new look. White, light gray, off-white, and pale neutrals convey the spirit of this efficient, uncluttered style. They are often used with sparse, simple accents of black, red, dark gray, or blue. Ornament is not eliminated but it is minimized and streamlined.

Another new approach is to exaggerate the use of colors and patterns in kaleidoscopic designs. Instead of the delicate florals and garlands of traditional designs, these bold contemporary tile designs focus on grids, squares, checks, diamonds, and stripes.

Contemporary designs also emphasize the functionality of ceramic tile. Because frost resistance, durability, cleanability, and slip resistance are of primary importance, tiles are selected on these characteristics.

There are many different types of contemporary tiles that work well in sleek, modern interiors. Unadorned or boldly patterned glazed wall tiles, quarry tiles, paver tiles, and mosaics can all be used in this setting.

▲ 93 This avant-garde living room lacks the dullness and sterility found in much of modern architecture. White glazed tiles and white painted walls act as a backdrop to the fresh pastel tones of the new wave furnishings and accessories.

▲ 94

Los Angeles Kaleidoscope

In a virtual explosion of pattern and color, this Los Angeles penthouse demonstrates a fresh approach to designing with ceramic tile. Tile is the predominant finish material used throughout the home—on walls, floors, stairs, countertops, and ceilings. Often, it is used in unique and surprising combinations. Glazed tile is most commonly used, since it provides the greatest range of color from which to work.

The kitchen is a favorite room, reminiscent of both an Art Deco diner and an Aztec shrine. Typical tile patterns include check, chevron, and stepped pyramid, providing an explosion of rhythm in the space. The

monochromatically tiled ceiling, sleek stainless steel cabinets, and commercial glass refrigerator provide soothing contrast. The brilliant red-tiled window frame also provides visual relief since it draws the eye to the outdoors.

The curving staircase includes an interesting juxtaposition of tile patterns installed on the stair risers. Checks, stepped pyramids, and diamond shapes create the colorful composition that acts as the focal point for the room. Tiled area rugs in quilt patterns surround the stair of this unusual contemporary home. Fifties' style accessories complete the design of the space.

▲ 96

Classic Nineties Bath

This small, multiuse bath models the ideals and lifestyle of the nineties. It provides both efficiency and privacy for adults, children, and guests in its function as the master bath, children's bath, and powder room. Ceramic tile was selected for beauty, durability, and ease of maintenance in this high-traffic, high-profile space.

Though the room is contemporary in function, classic details are used in creative ways. Sleek, large-scale tiles lend a clean and expansive feeling to the space. Pink grout and gray accents add a touch of color without cluttering the design. Natural light and a cloud-motif ceiling paper further expand the visual dimensions of the bath.

▲ 98

Contemporary Cottage

The traditional cottage theme is modernized and streamlined in this contemporary cottage home in suburban Los Angeles. Instead of the typical dark, cluttered, cottage look, this updated version emphasizes daylight, the views, and the vertical dimensions of the space. It also incorporates a sophisticated palette of finish materials including leather, iron, quartz, and glass mosaic tiles.

Sheathed in 1" x 1" Venetian or square glass tiles, the elegant built-in buffet table traverses the length of the peaked end wall. Both the tabletop and bullnose edge are clothed in these tiny mosaics, adding texture and just enough visual interest to the design. The subtle coloration of the pale green tiles mimics the hues of the garden and sky beyond. This allows the juxtaposition of windows, beams, and mirror to dominate the space.

Chapter 4

Ideas for Kitchens

*T*he kitchen is the working center of the home, the most used room and therefore the most important. It is the place where meals are prepared and food is stored, but it is much more significant than this definition implies. Kitchens also function as the family office, the bulletin board, the workshop, the pet feeding area, an entertainment space, and an informal dining area. Calendars, report cards, children's drawings, potted herbs, family pictures, and the cat's saucer are equally components of the extended function of the kitchen.

Beyond functional definitions, the kitchen is a symbolic space; embodying the home, warmth, safety, and the joys and pleasures of eating. Family and friends congregate to enjoy casual meals in these appealing spaces, and a well designed kitchen invites us to linger in its comfort and warmth. Both the body and spirit are renewed in kitchens, adding richness and depth to our lives.

Since the kitchen is the most used room of the house, it naturally receives the heaviest wear. Finishes for floors, countertops, walls, and—to a lesser extent—ceilings, must be selected with care. It is important to choose finishes that will resist intense foot traffic, sharp knives, hot pans, spills, mild acids, cleaning solutions, water, and airborne grease. Functional characteristics such as durability, slip resistance, chemical resistance, and stain resistance must also be considered for each of these surfaces. Selecting finishes with these characteristics will help ensure that the kitchen is efficient, since a good choice will minimize the cleanup work. Costly replacement of worn floors and countertops is also minimized when appropriate materials are selected.

Ceramic tile is particularly suitable for kitchens because of its dual characteristics of function and beauty. In kitchens, consider not only the beauty of a certain tile but also its functional characteristics and the manufacturer's recommendations for use. Aesthetically, the decision to use color, pattern, and texture should be weighed against the kitchen's method of storage and the location of cabinets and windows, as well as the juxtaposition of utensils, accessories, and appliances. Kitchens with open shelving have a cluttered, busy appearance that can be toned down by using restraint in the selection of tile pattern and color. In such cases, a simple monochromatic tile design will unify and balance the sometimes chaotic effect. Similarly, traditional fitted kitchen cabinets work well with fruit and vegetable patterns of decorative tiles and murals. The effect is both charming and visually interesting.

Often, kitchen and tile designs should relate in style to adjoining rooms in the house. Ceramic floor tiles used throughout several rooms can easily perform this function by visually linking and unifying the spaces. Both glazed and unglazed floor tiles work well in this application, each offering certain advantages for stain resistance and for durability.

The Heart of the Family

The values of the 1990s place increasing importance on family, home, and a simpler way of life. Along with these changes, there is a new perception of the role of the kitchen in the home. Kitchens are more important and are evolving into family rooms or living rooms. Friends and family gravitate to

▲ 100 A tiled pot rack and countertops accent the dark oak cabinetry in this traditional family kitchen. the rich stone-look floor tile adds an old-world ambiance while meeting the service demands of a large family.

these spaces for their lived-in, relaxed ambiance. Space for an easy chair, sofa, and fireplace are often included in the plans. Kitchen layouts for appliances and work surfaces allow for two or more cooks working in the kitchen at once. Personal touches and family treasures are also lovingly displayed in these comfortable, homey spaces.

The need for efficiency and modern conveniences is not forgotten in homey, family-centered kitchens. In fact, the contrary is true, because these kitchens are such well-loved and well-used spaces. Since homey kitchens don't sacrifice practicality for charm, ceramic tile is one of the best ways to ensure that the requirements for both function and ambiance are met. Ceramic tile walls, backsplashes, countertops, and floors are commonly used throughout these kitchens. Even stoves, vent hoods, and window sills can be sheathed in tile, making it the predominant material in the space.

Handmade, hand-glazed tiles are one of the best ingredients for creating a homey kitchen. These tiles have a simple, unpretentious look that adds a charming, old-world ambiance to the space. Mexican, Spanish, and Portuguese hand-painted decorative tiles depicting fruit, vegetables, and birds have an artless quality that is perfect for homey kitchens. They may be used either sparingly, or liberally, in conjunction with plain tiles, border tiles, and moldings of coordinated colors and sizes. Careful placement of each tile is necessary to create a tile design that is pretty but not overwhelming.

An elegant, yet charming, kitchen can be created with ceramic tile murals. Floral and cornucopia designs are most commonly used, but murals depicting fish, rabbits, or pheasants can whimsically appear to be the main ingredient for the evening meal. Murals require a planned approach to the design of the kitchen. A delicate balance must be struck among the tile, cabinets, appliances, and other features in the room.

For kitchen floors, large rustic tiles work best to create a cozy, casual atmosphere. Quarry tiles and terra cotta tiles impart this feeling of warmth and earthiness. Even some glazed floor tiles are suitable for the kitchen, depending on the appearance of the surface. Since many homey kitchens are quite large, darker floor tiles should be used to make the space feel more intimate. Dusty reds, browns, and golden terra cotta are cozy and also resist showing dirt. An added advantage is that many of these tiles are long-wearing and work well in high-traffic kitchens.

The color scheme for homey kitchens should be subtle and easy on the eye. Color schemes using beige, peach, brown, or rust add a warm, romantic feeling to the space. Cool tile colors such as blue and white are also traditional for these kitchens and can be used alone or as accents. For example, terra cotta floors sometimes employ glazed blue tiles as accents.

Gourmet Sophistication

Gourmet kitchens borrow ideas from professional kitchens with their no-nonsense, functional approach to design. These kitchens have a sleek, high-tech atmosphere and are equipped with the latest gadgetry and modern conveniences. Busy chefs are able to produce large amounts of food in these domestic workshops, since appliances, utensils, and ingredients are organized to be close at hand. Usually, the gourmet kitchen is separated from the living and dining spaces, since it lacks coziness and is intended for serious, uninterrupted cooking. Occasionally, a casual dining area will be located within these working kitchens if the cook likes to talk with guests while preparing meals.

Gourmet kitchens emphasize efficiency and hygiene when determining the layout and selection of cabinetry and finishes. Because every available surface is covered with pots, pans, and utensils, the use of closed, fitted cabinetry minimizes the clutter and contributes the appearance of tidiness when the kitchen is not in use. Some open shelving is available for frequently used cooking ingredients such as spices, herbs, and dried beans and pastas. Finish materials are valued for their durability and ease of maintenance, making ceramic tile a popular choice. Ceramic tile walls, countertops, and floors help the chef to concentrate on cooking, since these tile surfaces are relatively carefree and long-wearing.

Machinemade ceramic tiles convey the essence of the gourmet kitchen. Their crisp, clean lines impart an austere, industrial feeling that counteracts the organized chaos of preparing gourmet meals. Geometry is emphasized by these rigidly uniform tiles that create a streamlined, uncluttered look. Small and large, glazed and unglazed machinemade tiles are appropriate for this application. Glazed wall tiles, porcelain pavers, glazed pavers, and mosaics work particularly well since they are precise and uniform in appearance. When sheathing both walls and floors, polished porcelain pavers add understated elegance and sophistication to gourmet kitchens.

White is the most popular tile color for gourmet kitchens. White tiles seem coolly efficient and functional and counteract the busyness of these hardworking spaces. Moreover, white rectangular tiles add to this feeling of efficiency when installed vertically on walls. They seem to march along with machinelike efficiency. Since dirt, grease, and fingerprints are not masked by color, white tiles are easy to keep clean. They also reflect the light and add an open, airy feeling to the space.

Because any touch of color stands out in a white-tiled kitchen, use care in placing color. Walls and backsplashes are the best location for colored tile

▲ 101-102 Both stainless steel and ceramic tile are obvious choices for this sophisticated yet hardworking gourmet kitchen. The harlequin-motif backsplash is created from stone-look glazed tiles.

▶ 102

accents, since they add interest without cluttering the work surface. Borders, checkerboards, and stripes can be created with mosaics or glazed wall tiles. The patterning is best when it is simple, elegant, and geometric. Black, gray, blue, and red mosaics work particularly well when placed in a field of gleaming white tiles.

The Small Kitchen

A thoughtful, studied approach is necessary when designing small kitchens. All the elements of a larger kitchens must be included in a limited space: stove, oven, microwave, sink, refrigerator, countertops, and storage. Even if small kitchens require compromise in the use and placement of these elements, one should not compromise on the selection of finish materials. When properly designed, small kitchens are also hardworking kitchens, so that finish materials must be practical and long-wearing. The finish materials should also be carefully considered to prevent a cluttered appearance. Materials for walls, countertops and floors can serve to visually enlarge a small space by making the walls appear to recede.

Usually, small kitchens should match the style of adjoining rooms. This approach makes the kitchen feel larger, since it is aesthetically linked to the rest of the house. Minimalist designs work best since they are inherently streamlined, and the small kitchen will seem open and airy. Sleek, glazed floor tiles that continue through several rooms will add to this effect. Victorian and cottage kitchen themes can also work nicely, but some traditional details may need to be minimized or eliminated. Hand-painted stencils, busy checkerboard fabrics, and carved wood moldings must match the scale of the room and not overwhelm the space. In rustic, country kitchens the selection of roughened, irregular materials may be used sparingly in combination with smooth, sleek finishes. Handmade terra cotta floor tiles and smooth plaster walls create an appealing look for a quaint kitchen.

Ceramic tile is an excellent choice for small kitchens since the scale of the tile adds interest without overpowering the small space. Tile can even be used to make the kitchen appear larger and more spacious. One method is to use tile to draw the eye to the outdoors by placing tile adjacent to a glass door. A tile floor that extends from the kitchen through a French door to the adjacent patio, visually connects the two spaces and adds an unbroken spaciousness. Often, golden-brown or red quarry tiles are used to represent the earth and further merge the two spaces. Another idea is to frame windows with brightly colored mosaics or patterned decorative tiles. These accent tiles serve to highlight the view and draw your attention to the space beyond.

▲ 103 The predominant use of white visually enlarges this small kitchen. Rope moldings and an inset of diagonal tiles add subtle interest to the countertop and backsplash.

Light tiles and shiny glazed or polished tiles work well in small kitchens, since they reflect the light and give an open, airy feeling to the space. This effect is emphasized when the tiles are used on both walls and floors, creating a monolithic look. Darker, more dramatic tiles can be used as accents or as flooring in a small, rustic kitchen.

Tile patterns should be simple and uncomplicated, using a grout color that closely matches the field tile. This approach deemphasizes the grout lines and prevents a busy appearance. Decorative tiles and murals can also be used, but be careful not to overpower the space. Place them sparingly, with thought to other visually weighty objects such as windows and large appliances.

Creating Character

Many newer homes constructed in recent decades lack character and distinction. Their rooms, including the kitchen, lack the rich architectural details of the past, and are often boxlike, featureless spaces. In addition, these rooms lack a substantial, permanent feeling since inexpensive resilient floor coverings and plastic laminates are often used.

However, there is one advantage to a characterless space: it provides a blank canvas on which to work. Extensive demolition is not usually necessary and new finishes can often be installed over the old ones. Typical existing finishes such as walls painted in white or beige, sheet vinyl floors, and plastic laminate countertops can be replaced with new finishes that are alive with color, texture, and pattern.

It is easy to build new features into characterless kitchens, sheathing these new elements in tile. For example, a wall- or ceiling-mounted vent hood can be framed-in and covered in ceramic tile murals or decorative tiles. A tiled vent hood has a unique, sculptural quality that creates interest, becoming a natural focal point in the room. It can also add continuity to the design of the kitchen, since matching tiles can also be placed on the countertops or backsplash. Another possibility is to enhance an existing window by framing it with decorative border tiles to add interest, and draw the eye to the outdoors. Or, one can deepen the window sill, add tile and create an eye-catching, sunny spot for indoor flowers and herbs. Coffered ceilings, bulkheads, island worksurfaces, and open shelving can all be added to featureless kitchens and then sheathed in the glowing colors of ceramic tile.

Ceramic tile is one of the best ways to turn a nondescript kitchen into a unique and distinctive space. Any type of ambiance can be created for a feeling of coziness, sleekness, elegance, or hospitality. Checkerboard mosaic tile

▲ 104-105 This one-of-a-kind kitchen derives its personality from the funky, hand-painted fish and checkerboard tile designs. Additional character is created by framing the window in tile, thereby accenting the view and emphasizing the arched opening.

floors and Victorian floral, decorative wall tiles evoke a simpler, bygone era. Glossy, monochromatic glazed wall tiles and smooth glazed pavers create a sleek, contemporary look. In addition, antique floor tiles and rustic hand-made tiles can be used to add a comfortable, lived-in quality to the room. Each of these schemes adds richness, personality, and a sense of permanency to the kitchen.

▲ 105

Chapter 5

Ideas for Baths

*T*he bathroom performs an important role in our lives, and aside from the kitchen, is the most heavily used space in a home. Both mornings and evenings, bathing, grooming, and dressing are performed within the bathroom's private walls. The ritual of bathing goes back to Greek and Roman traditions, although privacy was much less important. Instead, the ancients bathed in elaborate public facilities for social interaction, relaxation, and simple hygiene.

The history of the modern bathroom begins with the Victorians. In fact, we owe them the invention of indoor plumbing, plumbed bathtubs, shower enclosures, and the water closet or toilet. By the late 1880s, Victorian bathrooms were planned as a separate room inside the house, often called the "necessary room." In its early development, the "necessary room" was a cramped and purely functional space that lacked comfort and luxury. Later, exuberant Victorian désigners embellished the space with ornate brass fittings, freestanding claw-foot tubs, and pedestal sinks. A ceramic tile floor and Persian carpet were also standard amenities.

Today, changes in lifestyle have forged a new role for the bathroom. Two-paycheck households and the added pressures of modern life require a place for relaxation and solitude. Incredibly, the bathroom is one of the few places we can still make this demand! Drawing upon Japanese influences, today's bathrooms have become a place for sanctuary, tranquility, and self-indulgence. They are more spacious, have additional amenities, and are both physically and psychologically therapeutic. Steam rooms, whirlpool baths, skylights, dressing tables, and double sinks add to the comfort of these spaces. This self-indulgent luxury invites us to linger and pamper ourselves in these enjoyable and intimate rooms.

Today's lifestyle has also developed different types of baths that serve various functions in a home. The private bath, guest bath, master bath, family bath, and powder room are a few examples. These rooms are tailored to meet the needs of specific user groups through size, location, layout, and amenities. Beyond these more common examples, baths have also developed into spas with room for an exercise bike, rowing machine, barbells, tanning booth, and sauna. Convenience is served since exercise occurs adjacent to the shower and sink. The bath as a lounge is another new theme. A sitting area, fireplace, private patio, television, and VCR allow the owner to relax, read or watch movies in complete privacy and comfort.

Since today's bathroom is no longer a purely utilitarian space, its style and ambiance reflect the change. Sterile decor, bland, colorless materials, and harsh lighting are left behind and replaced with a harmonious design. This most personal of rooms should reflect the unique character, tastes, and preferences of the owner.

Ceramic tile is the classic finish for bathrooms and an excellent way to add character and style. Its appeal has not been diminished by recent changes in bathrooms. Instead, many new tiles have been created to meet the increased demand for individual expression. Tile is no longer used just to keep the walls and floors dry, but rather, it is used to create a total design scheme. Tile manufacturers make this concept easy, since both wall and floor tiles are often color-coordinated with tubs, sinks, and toilets. Moldings and trim pieces also coordinate and can be used to create architectural features and rich, ornate details. Mirrors can be framed with elaborate tile moldings for a built-in, custom look. Ceramic chair rails, wainscots, and crown moldings can add interest to walls and tub surrounds. Decorative tiles, murals, and the wide range of colors, sizes, shapes, and textures of tile can all be used to create a unique, harmonized look for any bath.

When selecting tiles for bathroom floors, durability, maintenance, and slip resistance should be carefully considered. Many bathroom floors are subject to heavy foot traffic, strong cleaning solutions, and frequent water spills, so that floor tiles must be sufficiently durable and scratch-, chemical-, and slip-resistant. (See pages 37, 38, and 41 for additional information on durability, slip resistance, and maintenance.) These floors may be finished with either glazed or unglazed paver tiles, but shower floors should always employ unglazed tile to prevent slipping. Unglazed mosaic tiles are the best choice for showers since they are inherently slip-resistant, and the many grout lines add additional protection for wet, bare feet. Floor mats should also be used to help insure that feet are relatively dry before stepping on the tile floor.

Bathroom countertops also require special consideration since they must withstand spills of fingernail polish remover, makeup, and other toiletries. Glazed wall tiles are an excellent choice, providing the glaze can withstand these chemicals. The tile manufacturer's recommendations for use and laboratory test results will aid you in determining the appropriateness of the glaze for this application.

The Private Bath

The private bath is the most intimate of bathrooms. It is a space for either a single adult or a couple, but not for children or guests. The private bath is a very personal space, located adjacent to the bedroom and sometimes known in genteel terms as the boudoir bath. The intimacy of this room suggests that the decoration should closely reflect the owner's tastes and personal style. The owner's preferences are also reflected in the choice of ameni-

▲ 106-107 The classic charm of a 1930s bathroom is updated with tile, creating an opulent retreat for a modern gentleman. Brilliant new, cobalt blue, glass mosaics and shimmering bands of gold tiles set off the original white-tiled walls.

ties, including finish materials, plumbing fixtures, exercise and spa equipment, and sitting areas.

The private bath is also a well-used room. The old adage, "cleanliness is next to godliness" is still applicable to the hygienic habits of Americans, and the private bath is the primary location for scrubbing, showering, deodorizing, and soaking. Since many hours are spent within these steamy walls, finish materials must be easily maintained, resisting water, mildew, soap scum, and harsh cleaning solutions. Ceramic tile is the most sensible choice since it stands up to the all these demands. Hardworking floors, walls, countertops, tub surrounds, showers, whirlpools, Roman tubs, even ceilings—all benefit from the application of long-wearing ceramic tile.

The private bath has as many amenities as the owner can afford, with upscale ceramic tiles at prices ranging up to $40.00 per square foot. Floors, walls, countertops, and ceilings are often swathed in tile in many different luxurious decorating styles. Marbleized and metallicized tiles, decorative tiles and borders, moldings and murals offer expensive, high-end looks that can be traditional, contemporary, country, Victorian, or eclectic. Tile designs that imitate granite, limestone, and wood are also available with rich textures and surface pattern. Hand-painted faux mosaic tiles can also be used to create charming, antiquated looks that are the height of fashion in the 1990s.

Ceramic artists can also be employed to create one-of-a-kind tile designs for the opulent private bath. These original tiles are usually hand-painted, but silkscreen designs and decals are also produced. Custom mosaic murals are another possibility for adding originality to the room. Elaborate mosaic seascapes, florals, or water symbols can add spice to an otherwise typical bath. Intricate mosaic portraits can be used to imbue the room with a classical theme, reminiscent of opulent ancient Roman bathhouses.

The tile color scheme for a private bathroom should coordinate with the colors in the adjacent master bedroom. This use of color visually ties the two spaces, creating a peaceful retreat within the home. The colors selected should be subtle and easy on the eye, adding to the feeling of sanctuary and relaxation. Aquatic colors in shimmering blues and greens are an excellent choice, since they express the characteristics of water and emphasize the ritual of bathing. Romantic pastels are also subtle and pretty, suggesting luxury and self-indulgence. Muted pinks, mauves, corals, and creams create a dreamy, sentimental ambiance in a private bath.

The Guest Bath

The guest bath is a communal space, designed to accommodate one or more guests, but usually not at the same time. It is a more public space than the private bath, and it should be treated in a way that visually describes this function. Guest baths should be pretty and more formal than the private bath, since they are "dressed-up" for company. Practicality is not as important, since the space is only used infrequently and extensive storage or indulgent luxury is unnecessary. Guest baths are also more modest in size and offer few luxurious amenities. A single lavatory, toilet, and bathtub are standard fixtures. Or the guest bath may sometimes be a mere half-bath, with space for only a lavatory and toilet.

Ceramic tile is one amenity that the guest bath should not do without. Tile is an excellent way to dress up the space and give a it a unique appeal far removed from the clinical second bathroom of the past. Tile floors, walls, countertops, and ceilings add imaginative detail, personality, and flair to the guest bath. Both contemporary and traditional styles can be created using ceramic tile.

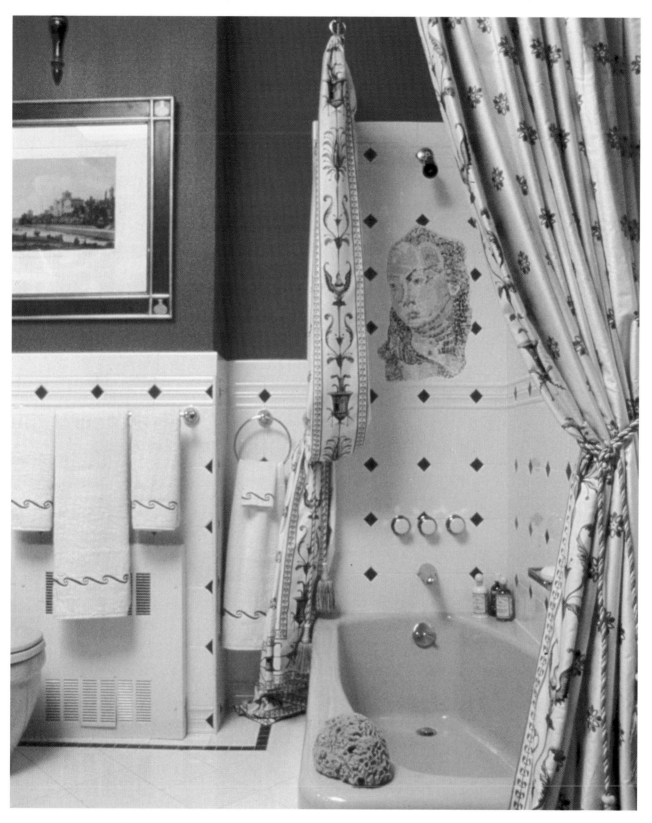

▲ 108-109 Dressed up for company, this stylish bath incorporates rich colors and classic patterns. In the shower, mosaic portraits of a woman's and man's face highlight each wall.

▲ 109

Period styles are a popular choice for guest baths. Handsome old fittings, rich mahogany cabinets, and brass hardware add an elegant old-world charm. Antique tiles can be used in conjunction with these traditional elements, since they contribute to the authenticity of the reproduction and complement the room's theme. Sometimes an entire countertop or wall is tiled in antique tiles; sometimes only antique decorative inserts are set in a field of new, monochromatic tiles. Fragile antique tiles work especially well in the guest bath, since they will not be exposed to heavy-duty use. New decorative tiles with designs of roses, vines, garlands, and bows offer additional references to the look of days past. These new tiles are usually less expensive and more readily available than antiques, yet are still able to enhance the old-world style of the room.

Often, the tile design of a guest bathroom should match the style of the adjacent rooms, adding continuity to the design of the house. If located off an elegant marbleized tile entry hall, the guest bath should carry this same floor tile into the space to create a unified look. The continuous tile flooring will enlarge the small space while adding elegance and sophistication. Color-coordinated wall tiles, plumbing fixtures, fabrics, and towels will complete the design of the room. If the guest bath is located off a carpeted space such as a bedroom, use coordinated tile colors and patterns to add unity to the design. These colors and patterns need not match exactly but may merely echo the look of the adjacent room.

In keeping with the dressy look of the guest bath, tile colors should be high-end or rich and romantic. Deep emerald green, burgundy, or dusty blues provide rich contrast to glowing, white porcelain fixtures. Muted pastels also work well, adding delicacy and romance to the space. Graphic black and white schemes create an exciting, upscale look that can be either traditional or contemporary in style.

The Small Bath

The bathroom is so common today that it is taken for granted as a standard modern convenience. Unfortunately, we must also assume that the existing bath of many homes is small and of mean proportions. In older homes, a cramped bath may be located under a staircase, while in newer homes a small second bath may be relegated to an unused corner of the basement. Often, it is not practical or affordable to increase the dimensions of these baths, so ingenuity is required to make the most of the existing area. The toilet, sink, bathtub, or shower and sufficient storage must be accommodated using every inch of precious space.

The minimalist aesthetic provides a workable model for the small bath. Whether Shaker style or high tech, small bathrooms benefit from the emphasis on simplicity and sleek, functional lines. A tiny bathroom will seem even more cramped with the clutter of several finish materials of varying colors, patterns, and textures. In contrast, a streamlined, minimalist design scheme will disguise the limited space. The deft use of pale, monochromatic colors, mirrors, lighting, and uniform ceramic tiles will also visu-

▲ 110 This small but stately bathroom is visually enlarged by the predominant use of white. Handmade relief tiles and moldings, in muted shades of green, add richness to the space.

ally expand the area. Depending on the style of the room, both machine-made and handmade tiles may be appropriate.

Connecting the small bath to the outdoors is another method of visually enlarging the space. If possible, add French doors that open onto a secluded outdoor garden and extend floor tiles from the bath into the exterior space. This will greatly enlarge the feel of the room and allow sun worshipers to linger in the morning light. If this is not possible, take advantage of a view and draw the eye to the outdoors, increasing the perspective in the space. Windows framed in brightly colored or patterned tile will greatly emphasize the view.

The small bath is often the only bath for a household and therefore must function as both the family bath and guest bath. Adults, teenagers, children, guests, and even pets must all be accommodated in this well-used and hardworking space. Finish materials for the space must be equally hardworking, making ceramic tile the practical choice. Glazed wall tiles, glazed mosaics, and glazed paver tiles are especially easy to keep clean since they can be washed down with minimal effort. Unglazed mosaics, quarry tiles, terra cotta, and paver tiles are also appropriate, since they are durable enough to handle the demands of a large family.

Ceramic tile is an excellent choice for small bathrooms as it can be used to enlarge the meager space while creating a pleasing ambiance. Monolithic tile designs provide an expansive look that is also pleasing and sophisticated. In these schemes, walls, floors, and countertops are sheathed in the same size and color tile that is installed with a matching color of grout. Minimal pattern and light colors are used to intensify the effect. Since the tub is often the largest element in the room, its dominance can be minimized and balanced by sheathing it in tile as well.

Creating Character

It's easy to add character to a nondescript bathroom with the use of ceramic tile. Watercolored tiles, in varied hues of blue and green, have immediate impact, since they symbolize the ritual of cleansing. Marine themes with fish, mermaid, and seashell designs are also effective, often adding a fanciful or whimsical feeling to the room.

A more subtle and sophisticated approach is to add decorative ceramic tile moldings to walls. Place the moldings at chair rail height, or as a crown molding, with ceramic tile sheathing the wall below. This method adds a feeling of depth and permanence to the space and can also add a focal point to the room by emphasizing the tub surround or shower wall. For additional impact, add decorative tiles or a mural to the wall you want to emphasize.

▲ 111-112 Water motifs are a favorite way to add character to baths. Here, a family bath sports whimsical sea creatures enjoyed by children and adults alike. Floors, countertops, and a Japanese-style soaking tub are all sheathed in these handmade tiles.

Perhaps the easiest way to add character to a bath is with tile color schemes that are precoordinated by the manufacturer. Several companies offer this arrangement with patterns and colors that you can mix and match to create an eye-pleasing yet personalized look. For example, combine check pattern tiles with delicate florals, pinstripes, or monochromatic tiles in color-coordinated schemes. Occasionally, these tiles are even designed to coordinate with other bathroom finishes and accessories such as wallpaper, plastic laminates, plumbing fixtures, and even towels. This arrangement offers additional depth to the design while simplifying the selection process.

▲ 112

Chapter *6*

Ideas for Other Spaces

*T*he versatility of ceramic tile allows its use in many spaces in a home—not just kitchens and baths. The many different colors, sizes, shapes, patterns, and textures of tile adapt well to living rooms, entries, sunrooms, fireplaces, patios, and pools. The complete spectrum of styles and design schemes can be enhanced with tile, whether it is a homey, country-style family room or an elegant, Federal-style foyer. After all, tile is so beautiful that it should not be hidden away in the utilitarian spaces of a home. And tile adds an enduring quality to these spaces while meeting their requirements for durability and ease of maintenance.

The beauty of tile cries out for its use in the most public spaces of a home. Welcome a visitor with ceramic tile address signage or decorative touches of tile surrounding the exterior face of windows and doors. Delight a thirsty guest with a drink served from a wet bar sheathed in decorative tiles. Or surprise a dinner party with a whimsical trompe l'oeil mural on the dining room wall.

Americans could do well to take a lesson from the Europeans, who commonly use tile throughout the home. On fireplaces, they use tile to add a unique, personalized touch, creating a focal point in the room. On patios, they use tile to extend the boundaries of the house to the outdoors, inviting the occupants to relax outdoors in comfort and style. Their hardworking entries and foyers make good use of tile's durability and low maintenance. And, in snowy areas, their tiled mud rooms are sometimes equipped with a drain. Muddy boots and shoes, as well as the tile floor, can be washed down easily and with no permanent stains or damage.

Exteriors especially benefit from the application of tile when pools and fountains have decorative touches of tile. These elements take on a unique, personalized style that harsh concrete cannot approach. The waterline of a pool is a great place to let your imagination go, using bright colors or bold and unusual patterns. Combine new tiles with antique tiles to add interest to a fountain wall or a unique backyard sundial. Remember that the play of light and shadow adds a new element to the design. Relief tiles take on a new look in the midday sun, while dark, shadowy areas can be brightened with glossy, glazed tiles that reflect and enhance the minimal light.

The Entry

The entry, or foyer, is the most public of spaces in a home. It welcomes the visitor, shelters the delivery man, and is the setting of the continual comings and goings of the occupants of the home. Needless to say, it is a well-used room, since it acts as a transition from the exterior and a prelude to the living room.

▲ 113 Black glazed floor tiles act as a background to the rich architectural details of this elegant foyer and stair. Functionally, the tile is an excellent choice for this high-traffic, high-maintenance space.

The design of the foyer sets the tone for the entire house and therefore, should be carefully thought out. Its design should relate to the adjacent spaces and should show off the home in its best light. For these reasons, foyers are a great place to flaunt the pattern and color of a beautiful ceramic tile floor. In a foyer many types of tile will work well—intricately detailed mosaics, dressy marbleized paver tiles, and earthy quarry tiles. The walls of foyers can also benefit from ceramic tiles. The Victorians often used decorative relief tiles to dress up the walls of this public space.

The unique conditions of a foyer also require that the floor must withstand heavy foot traffic, as well as tracked-in mud and dirt. The occasional blowing rainstorm may even cause the floor to become wet. Again, ceramic tile is a good choice here, as long as the selection is also governed by function. Select a tile that provides good slip resistance when wet and requires minimal maintenance. Cementitious grouts and the more porous unglazed tiles should be sealed to prevent staining in these areas.

The Living Room

The living room is perhaps the most social of all the spaces in a home. It is often the setting for both festive parties and quiet conversations with friends. It is a place to dress up and enjoy holidays and other special occasions with family and friends.

Living rooms take on a new—and much improved—character when typical wall-to-wall carpeting is replaced with ceramic tile. A tiled living room floor has an enduring, solid quality that gives the home a sense of history and permanence. Tile is also more sanitary than carpet, because spills, dust, and tracked-in dirt can be easily and completely removed. Another benefit is that tile is more ecologically friendly than carpet. Worn and stained carpets are regularly removed and replaced, as our burgeoning landfills bear out. In contrast, the longevity of tile eliminates the need for periodic replacement, so that there are ecological benefits from its use.

A fireplace is often located in the living room and is an excellent location for tile. A tiled fireplace stimulates the imagination while being a practical choice, since it is unaffected by extremes in temperature. Patterned decorative tiles and murals or monochromatic tiles work equally well, depending on the design and style of the room.

A wet bar is an important amenity to the living room and another logical place to install ceramic tile. When selecting tile for a wet bar, be sure to check with the manufacturer to determine if the tile will resist staining and etching of the glaze from alcohol, juice, soft drinks, and other spills.

◀ 114 The artless quality of this wet-bar stems from the use of hand-made turquoise tiles. The frieze molding treatment brings the design to life, adding interest and definition to the design.

◀ 115-116 Handmade tiles in muted greens and shimmering gold sheath the face and hearth of this Arts-and-Crafts–style fireplace.

▼ 116

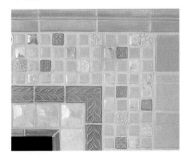

The Sunroom

The sunroom is an obvious location for application of ceramic tile. Tile permits the occasional spill when watering potted plants and has an earthy, natural feeling appropriate for the space. The heat retaining characteristics of tile also make it an excellent finish material for these sunny spaces. Passive solar designs often incorporate a tile floor set on a concrete substrate. The tile and concrete absorb heat during the day and radiate it into the space at night.

Vine and flower motifs are popular themes for decorative tiles in sunrooms. They mimic nature and create a calm, peaceful setting. Bird and animal designs are also appropriate and are often interspersed throughout a field of rustic terra cotta or quarry tiles on a large expanse of flooring.

▶ 117 Quarry tile is an excellent choice for sunrooms because of its earthy, natural appearance. The tile also absorbs and radiates heat in passive solar designs.

◀ 118 Tile turns a patio into an inviting outdoor room. Here, buff-colored paver tiles are set on the diagonal and accented with touches of blue.

◀ 119 This unique floral wreath mosaic identifies the owner's street address.

Pools and Fountains

Pools and fountains offer several locations that benefit from the application of ceramic tile: the pool deck, the waterline, and the floor of the pool or fountain. Because each of these applications makes unique demands on the tile, a thoughtful selection should be made.

Tiles exposed to the water in the pool are also exposed to the chlorine in the water. Since some glazed tiles will react adversely to this chemical, the manufacturer's recommendations for use should be followed. Tiles for the deck and pool steps have a different requirement, since bare, wet feet should be able to tread without slipping. As with patios, select unglazed tiles for these locations in lieu of the more slippery, glazed types.

▲ 120 Florals and monochromatic blue tiles highlight the waterline of this pool.

▲ 121 A multicolored school of fish darts through the depths of this magical pool. Handmade porcelain mosaics are used to create the intricate design.

▲ 122-123 A backyard is transformed into a soothing retreat with the addition of a green, tiled fountain. The fountain also masks a driveway located just beyond the back wall.

▼ 123

Stairs

Handsome and long-lasting, tile is an excellent choice for both interior and exterior stairs. Terra cotta, paver tiles, and quarry tiles are suitable for stair treads, while decorative tiles, glazed wall tiles, and even murals work well on stair risers.

The slip resistance of a tile is a primary concern when selecting tile for any stair, but especially an exterior stair. As exterior stairs are exposed to rain and ice, be sure to look for special tile treads with ribbing or added texture.

◀ 124 New decorative tiles, inspired by traditional California tilemakers, accent the risers of this beautiful outdoor stair.

◀ 125 New and antique tiles were used to create original murals on each of the four sides of this interesting sundial. Ceramic numerals are inlaid on the top of the sundial and are used to accurately tell the time.

▶ 126 Tile enlivens the walkways and door surround to this unusual home.

The Patio

Any area of paving surrounding a home will certainly benefit from the color, texture, and pattern of ceramic tile. Harsh, bare concrete patios, walkways, and even driveways are transformed with tile, becoming more like an outdoor room.

Obviously, exterior grade tiles should be used for these areas, and in freeze-thaw climates, a frost-resistant tile must be selected. Porcelain paver tiles, most quarry tiles, and some terra cotta tiles meet this criterion, but be sure that the manufacturer recommends this use. Glazed tiles should not be used since pedestrians could easily slip on the impervious surface coating.

Color selections for patios often mimic nature with warm, earthy browns and dusty reds with ivy green accents. Again, quarry tiles, terra cotta tiles, and porcelain tiles are popular choices.

Furniture

Tabletops offer the tile lover another means of expression through ceramic tile. This use of tile is especially popular for casual patio tables, but ornate dining tables and coffee tables are also available. Both painted techniques and mosaics are utilized to create stunning colors and patterns of tile.

◄ 127 Ceramic tabletops are both beautiful and functional. Here, an original tile design is set on a wrought-iron base.

Chapter *7*

Fundamentals

Installation

The careful selection of materials and methods for installation is just as important as the selection of the tile itself. Even the most durable tile will fail if the installation method is inappropriate for the unique conditions of its application. In recent years, many improvements have been made in installation materials and methods, and standards have been tested and approved by ANSI. The ANSI standard specifications for installation materials are detailed in the ANSI A118 series and A136.1; the installation methods are described in the ANSI A108 series.

An important guide for installation methods is the *Handbook for Ceramic Tile Installation* by the Tile Council of America (TCA). This handbook provides over 75 details or methods of installing tile on walls, floors, countertops, exteriors, showers, and steam rooms with all types of substrates and structural conditions. (A copy may be obtained through the TCA at the address listed in the Directory.)

The following general information provides sound installation practices with proven materials recommended by ANSI and TCA.

Initial Considerations

There are three major factors to consider when evaluating installation methods for a tile project: structural loading, deflection, and substrate condition. Each of these must be carefully researched and evaluated as they will affect the choice of setting materials, installation method, and long-term success of the installation.

Structural loading is an important consideration because of the weight of ceramic tile installations. This is especially true of thick-bed installations, since the cement bed increases the load on a structure by approximately 12 pounds per square foot for floor installations and 100 pounds per linear foot for wall installations. Most residential construction is designed for a live load of 40 pounds per square foot. Therefore, depending on the structural conditions, the thick-bed installation may be acceptable. If not, thin-set installations may be used, since they are much lighter and avoid overloading the structure. If you are in doubt of the load-bearing capacity of your building, an evaluation should be performed by a structural engineer. (Further explanation of thick-bed and thin-set installations is provided on pages 148 and 149.)

Excessive deflection, or bending of the subfloor, will destroy tile installations because ceramic tile and setting materials are usually rigid in nature and cannot accommodate bending stresses. Subfloors with deflections require the use of a thick-bed method over a cleavage membrane. A cleavage membrane of roofing felt or polyethylene film is placed between the subfloor and the setting bed and serves to isolate the tiles from the excessive movement. This method prevents the cracking and popping of the tiles that would occur if they were bonded directly to the subfloor. In residential construction, these floors can often be made acceptable by the addition of a layer of $3/4$" exterior grade plywood to build up the subfloor and decrease the deflection. Subfloors not subject to deflection may be set using a thin-set installation method. Latex–portland cement mortars or epoxies are generally suitable for these thin-set installations.

The condition of the substrate also affects the choice of installation materials and methods for both walls and floors. This includes factors such as dimensional irregularity, cracks, and foreign coatings. ANSI has established standards for the maximum allowable variation of substrate for the different types of installations. These are as follows:

FLOORS

Installation Method	*Max. Variation in the Substrate from Required Plane*
Thick-bed	$1/4$" in 10'–0"
Dry-set mortar or latex–portland cement mortar	$1/8$" in 10'–0"
Organic adhesive or epoxy adhesive	$1/16$" in 3'–0"
Epoxy mortar	$1/8$" in 10'–0"

WALLS

Thick-bed	$1/4$" in 8'–0"
Dry-set mortar or latex-portland cement mortar	$1/8$" in 8'–0"
Organic adhesive	$1/8$" in 8'–0"

Flooring substrates that do not meet these tolerances can accept tile installed using a thick-set method with a leveling coat. The leveling coat is applied to the subfloor to make it uniform. Likewise, wall substrates with excessive dimensional irregularity, cracking, or foreign coatings can accept tile installed using a thick-set method over metal lath.

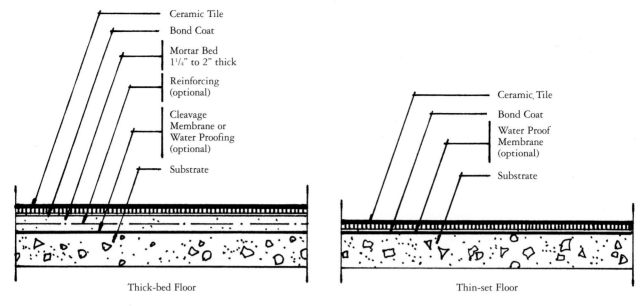

Ceramic Tile

Bond Coat

Mortar Bed
1¼" to 2" thick

Reinforcing
(optional)

Cleavage
Membrane or
Water Proofing
(optional)

Substrate

Thick-bed Floor

Ceramic Tile

Bond Coat

Water Proof
Membrane
(optional)

Substrate

Thin-set Floor

▲ 128

Materials and Methods for Installation

As indicated previously, there are two basic methods for installing tile: thick-bed and thin-set. Within these basic methods there are several variations using numerous types of installation materials. Mortar, adhesives, and grouts are manufactured with varying characteristics to meet the demands of most applications.

Thick-bed

Thick-bed installations are those in which the tiles are set on a thick mortar bed consisting of a mixture of sand and portland cement. Depending on the application, the mortar bed can be ³/₄" to 1" thick on walls and 1¼" to 2" thick on floors. Thick-bed installations are suitable for most applications unless the structural load capacity or space requirements do not permit their use. Thick-beds can be installed over waterproofing and cleavage membranes, and with reinforcing or metal lath to meet the requirements of the installation. Because of their thickness, some thick-beds can also be sloped to provide positive drainage of surface water.

Historically, thick-bed installations were the traditional method of installing tile. They are generally very durable and resistant to damage by water. However, thick-bed installations require more labor and are more expensive.

Thin-set

Thin-set installations are appropriately named because the tiles are attached directly to the substrate with a thin bond coat. Several types of materials may be used for the bond coat, including dry-set mortar, latex–portland cement mortar, epoxy mortar, modified epoxy emulsion mortar, epoxy adhesive, and organic adhesive. Depending on the type of material, the thin-set bond coat can be $^3/_{32}$" to $^1/_8$" thick.

Thin-set installations have several advantages over thick-bed. They weigh less, are faster to install, and require less space. Labor costs are also lower than with thick-bed installations.

Mortars and Adhesives

There are many types of mortars and adhesives, with varying technical characteristics as described below:

1. *Thick-bed, portland cement mortar* A mixture of portland cement and sand or portland cement, sand, and lime. The lime is only added for wall installations, since it makes the mixture adhere to the vertical surface. On some types of thick-bed mortars, absorptive ceramic tiles may need to be soaked in water before setting.

2. *Dry-set mortar* A mixture of portland cement, sand, and water retentive agents. Absorptive tiles set with dry-set mortar do not have to be soaked.

3. *Latex–portland cement mortar* A mixture of portland cement, sand, and latex additives. This mortar is similar to dry-set but has the advantage of higher bond strength, additional frost resistance, and greater flexibility. Usually, the liquid latex is used in place of water when mixing the material. However, dry latex formulations are also available that are activated by the addition of water.

4. *Epoxy mortar* A system employing 100 percent solids epoxy resin, filler, and epoxy hardner that can be used as a mortar or grout. Chemical resistance, stain resistance, high bond strength and water cleanup are the advantages to this material. Close attention should be paid to the manufacturer's instructions for mixing and cleanup.

5. *Modified epoxy emulsion mortar* A system employing epoxy resin and epoxy hardener with portland cement and sand that can be used as a mortar or grout. This mortar has high bond strength, is water-cleanable, and has improved chemical resistance over other portland-cement-based mortars.

Material costs are lower than those of epoxy mortar. Close attention should be paid to the manufacturer's instructions for mixing and cleanup.

6. *Epoxy adhesive*   An adhesive system employing epoxy resin and epoxy hardner. This material is similar to epoxy mortar, but usually is not as chemical resistant. As with all epoxies, close attention should be paid to the manufacturer's instructions for mixing and cleanup.

7. *Organic adhesive*   A one-part, ready-to-use adhesive for interior use only. Sometimes called mastic, organic adhesives are economical, easy to use, and provide adequate bond strength for most residential applications. They should not be used in wet areas or high-traffic floor areas.

Grouts

Grouts are materials used to fill the joints between tiles. Some grouts are available with and without sand. The sanded varieties are for use with ceramic mosaics, quarry tile, and pavers, since the grout lines are wider and the sand adds strength to the grout. Unsanded grouts are typically used with glazed wall tiles or with tiles with very narrow joints. This prevents scratching of the surface glaze and allows the grout to fit into the narrow grout line. A description of each of the basic grout types is as follows:

1. *Commercial portland cement grout*   A normally factory prepared, dense, portland-cement-based grout with water-resistant properties. This grout is available with or without sand. Damp curing is required.

2. *Sand–portland cement grout*   A site-mixed grout of portland cement, sand, and sometimes lime. The cement-to-sand ratio may be altered as necessary for the width of the grout line. Damp curing is required.

3. *Dry-set grout*   A normally factory prepared mixture of portland cement and water retentive agents. Tiles grouted with dry-set grout do not have to be soaked. They are available with and without sand.

4. *Latex-portland cement grout*   A mixture of portland cement and latex additives that is sometimes mixed with sand. This grout is similar to dry-set, but has the advantage of being less absorptive, and more flexible, and cures without damp curing. Usually, the liquid latex is used in place of water when mixing the material. However, dry latex formulations are also available that are activated by the addition of water.

5. *Epoxy grout*   A system employing 100 percent solids epoxy resin, filler, and epoxy hardener that can be used as a grout or mortar. Chemical resistance, stain resistance, high bond strength, and water cleanup are

the advantages to this material. Close attention should be paid to the manufacturer's instructions for mixing and cleanup.

6. *Modified epoxy emulsion grout* A system employing epoxy resin and epoxy hardener with portland cement and sand that can be used as a grout or mortar. This grout has high bond strength, is water-cleanable, and has improved chemical resistance over other portland-cement-based grouts. Material costs are lower than with epoxy grout. Close attention should be paid to the manufacturer's instructions for mixing and cleanup.

7. *Silicone rubber grout* An elastomeric grout system employing high-strength silicone rubber. This grout is resistant to water and stains, but should not be used for kitchen countertops unless the manufacturer specifically permits this type of use.

8. *Mastic grout* A one-part, ready-to-use grout. Mastic grouts are economical, easy to use, and provide good bond strength.

9. *Mildew-resistant grout* A portland-cement-based grout with fungicides added to the mixture. This grout inhibits the growth of mildew.

Steps of Installation

This section covers the general steps of installing ceramic tile. The following steps should familiarize the reader with basic installation processes and further explain the differences between thick-bed and thin-set installations. Both floor and wall installations are discussed.

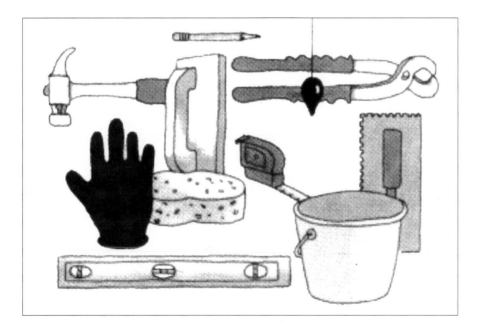

◀ 129 Tile-setting tools shown clockwise are as follows: rubber gloves, rubber mallet, hard rubber float, pencil, nippers, chalk line, notched trowel, bucket, tape measure, sponge, and carpenter's level.

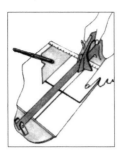

▲ 130 A tile cutter is used to score the tile and snap the pieces apart.

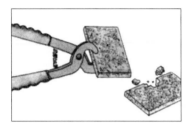

▲ 131 Use nippers to make curved or rounded cuts.

▲ 132 Comb the mortar using the notched side of the trowel to achieve an even setting bed.

▲ 133 Use a rubber mallet and beating block to beat in the tiles.

Thick-bed Installations

FLOORS

Substrate preparation

- Remove old floor coverings such as paint, resilient tiles, seamless flooring, and hardwood flooring, if possible. Glossy or painted surfaces that cannot be easily removed should be roughened by sanding or scarifying, or a new substrate may be installed over the existing flooring. (This step is not necessary if using a cleavage membrane.) Clean the surface to eliminate dust and loose material. (*Warning*: Asbestos tiles and lead paints are not readily identifiable and may cause serious physical harm if removed or roughened.)

- Install a cleavage membrane and reinforcing mesh to floors that have excessive deflection.

- Install a waterproofing membrane and reinforcing mesh to floors that are subject to standing water. Waterproof membranes are available in several types, including built-up, single-ply, liquid, or flexible sheet.

- Install a leveling coat to floors that have more than $^1/_4$" in 10'-0" variation in slab.

Tile preparation

- Highly absorptive tiles should be soaked in clean water and allowed to drain if installed on a plastic mortar bed. Consult the manufacturer regarding proper installation techniques of absorptive tiles.

- Inspect tiles for defects and improper shading prior to installation. Open several cartons in order to select and install tile that has been blended from several cartons. Provide adequate lighting during installation.

Layout

- Determine the best layout that centers the tile at the focal point of the room or minimizes cuts in the tile.

Laying the tiles

- Apply a thin coat of pure portland cement slurry to the properly prepared substrate if a cleavage membrane or waterproof membrane is not used.

- Immediately apply the portland cement and sand mortar to a small portion of the floor and level. The thickness should be between $1^1/_4$" and 2". Continue applying the mortar in small sections until the entire floor is covered.

- Install the bond coat in one of two ways: 1) apply neat cement or dust portland cement over a mortar bed that is still plastic, or 2) allow the mortar bed to cure and use dry-set, latex–portland cement, epoxy, or organic adhesives.

- Press tiles into the bond coat with appropriate spacing, using a slight twisting motion. Vibrating and backbuttering may be necessary to obtain total coverage for large dimension tiles. Cut tiles where necessary to fit the dimensions of the room. Tamp the tiles to level.

▲ 134 Remove excess grout by using the float as a squeegee applied in a diagonal direction across the surface of the tiles.

Grouting

- Working a small area at a time, force grout into the spaces between the tiles with a rubber float, using a diagonal motion across the tiles. Depending on job site conditions, wait approximately ten minutes and clean the surface with a damp terry cloth in a diagonal motion. (*Note:* Some absorptive, unglazed tiles may require the use of grout release to aid in the removal of grout from the face of the tile. Consult the tile manufacturer for installation instructions.)

Curing

- Damp cure and cover tile with heavy-duty construction paper to prevent staining of the grout. Avoid traffic across the installation for several days or protect with boards laid over walkways.

▲ 135 After letting joints harden, pull a flat damp towel diagonally across the surface of the tiles, from corner to corner, to remove grout residue.

WALLS

Thick-bed walls are installed in a similar manner to floors. Lime is added to the portland cement and sand to make the mixture adhere to the walls. A metal lath should be applied to the structure and used as a substrate over irregular, cracked, or coated surfaces or over metal and wood studs.

Thin-set Installations

FLOORS

Substrate Preparation

- As with bonded thick-bed installations, care should be taken to remove old floor coverings such as paint, resilient tiles, seamless flooring, and hardwood flooring, if possible. Glossy or painted surfaces that cannot be easily removed should be roughened by sanding or scarifying, or a new substrate may be installed over the existing flooring. Clean the surface to eliminate dust and loose material. (*Warning:* Asbestos tiles and lead

▲ 136 After the grout has dried, remove remaining haze from the surface of the tiles, using a slightly damp scouring pad.

paints are not readily identifiable and may cause serious physical harm if removed or roughened.)

- Install a waterproofing membrane to floors that are subject to standing water. Waterproof membranes are available in several types, including built-up, single-ply, liquid, or flexible sheet.

Tile preparation

- Inspect tiles for defects and improper shading prior to installation. Open several cartons in order to select and install tile that has been blended from several cartons. Provide adequate lighting during installation.

Layout

- Determine the best layout that centers the tile at the focal point of the room or minimizes cuts in the tile.

Laying the tiles

- Apply the thin-set mortar to a small portion of the floor with a notched trowel using the flat side first, then the notched side.

- Press tiles into the thin-set mortar with the appropriate spacing, using a slight twisting motion. Vibrating and backbuttering may be necessary to obtain total coverage for large dimension tiles. Cut tiles where necessary to fit the dimensions of the room. Tamp the tiles to level.

Grouting

- Working a small area at a time, force grout into the spaces between the tiles with a rubber float using a diagonal motion across the tiles. Depending on job site conditions, wait approximately ten minutes and clean the surface with a damp terry cloth in a diagonal motion. (*Note:* Some absorptive, unglazed tiles may require the use of grout release to aid in the removal of grout from the face of the tile. Consult the tile manufacturer for installation instructions.)

Curing

- Damp cure and cover tile with heavy duty construction paper to prevent staining of the grout. Avoid traffic across the installation for several days or protect with boards laid over walkways.

WALLS

Thin-set walls are installed in a similar manner to thin-set floors. The layout of wall tile is critical to provide a professional appearance. Sometimes the first row of tiles is at the bottom of the wall and the installation proceeds up the wall. At other times, the first row is at the ceiling with the cut tiles at the bottom.

Expansion Joints

Expansion joints are crucial to the success of tile installations. They provide flexible joints in tilework that allow for the expansion of the floor or wall. According to the *Handbook for Ceramic Tile Installation,* "expansion joints are required where tilework abuts restraining surfaces such as the perimeter walls, dissimilar floors, curbs, columns, pipes, ceilings, and where changes occur in backing materials." The handbook also requires that "all expansion, control, construction, cold, and seismic joints in the structure should continue through the tilework." Omission of these flexible joints may cause cracking of the tile or loss of bond, since the expansion forces are not properly relieved.

The location of expansion joints are the responsibility of the architect and should be designated on the construction documents. In larger buildings, expansion joints must be located at regular intervals. The TCA recommends the following:

Interior: 24' to 36' in each direction

Exterior: 12' to 16' in each direction

(Note: Interiors that are exposed to direct sunlight or moisture should have expansion joints located 12' to 16' in each direction.)

Surface Bullnose

Trim Tiles

Trim tiles are tiles with special shapes that finish off the edges of tile installations. They provide a clean, finished edge at locations where the tile stops and another finish begins. This juxtaposition often occurs at the top of a wainscot or the side of a tiled tub enclosure. Trim tiles are also used to allow tile installations to go easily around corners. These corners occur in most installations, and are located at the connections between walls and floors, at the front edge of countertops, and at unframed openings in walls.

Trim comes in a wide variety of shapes, sizes, and colors to match most types of ceramic tile. Glazed wall tile, ceramic mosaics, paver tiles, and quarry tiles all have matching trim tiles. Because of the differences in installation methods, two basic types of trim are manufactured: conventional trim and surface trim.

Conventional Bullnose

▲ 137

COMMON TRIM TILES

Thin-set Shapes   Thick-bed Shapes

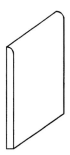

Bullnose

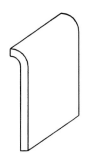

Bullnose

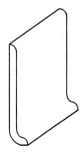

Thin-Lip Base

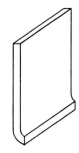

Cove Base

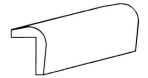

Counter Trim

Glazed Wall Tile

Bullnose

Cove

Cap

Ceramic Mosaics

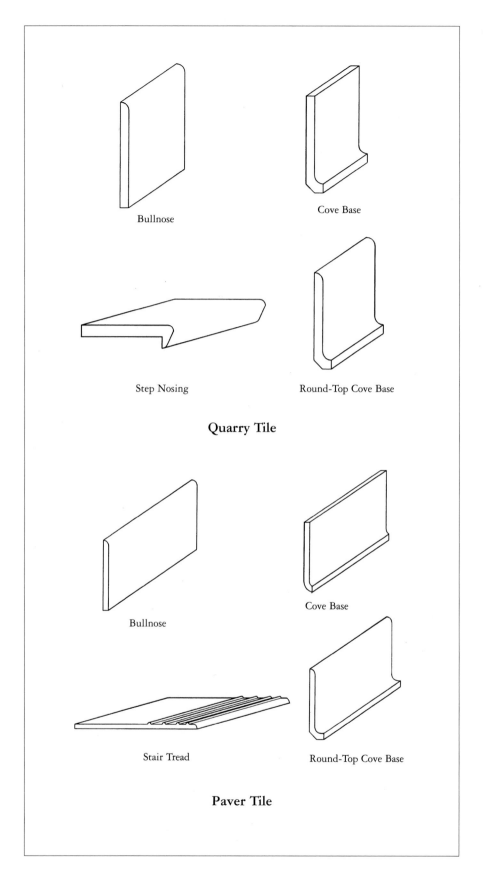

Bullnose

Cove Base

Step Nosing

Round-Top Cove Base

Quarry Tile

Bullnose

Cove Base

Stair Tread

Round-Top Cove Base

Paver Tile

Conventional trim is trim with radius curves designed for use in mortar bed or thick-bed installations. In these installations, the setting bed is thick, causing it to sit above the surrounding surface. The radius curves of these trim tiles permit the tile to curve around the setting bed and cover the edges of the thick mortar bed. An example of this condition occurs in mud-set wainscots, where the wall tile sits out approximately ³/₄" from the untiled portion of the wall above. A radius bullnose is used to finish the top edge of the wainscot, since it curves around to meet the surrounding wall. Many types of conventional trim are manufactured including radius bullnose, double bullnose, cove base, and quarter round.

Surface trim tiles are similar to conventional trim except that they have rounded edges instead of curves. They are essentially flat, with one or more rounded edges. Surface trim is used for installations where the setting bed is thin and the tile sits flush with the surrounding surface. As with conventional trim, many types of surface trim are available for most installations. The drawings on pages 156 and 157 demonstrate the most common shapes available.

There are some types of tile that do not have matching trim tile, such as thick, soft-bodied terra cotta floor tiles. Occasionally, manufacturers will not make trim in some lines of glazed wall tile, ceramic mosaics, pavers, and quarry tile. In these cases, substitutes can be made by using an accent tile for the trim shape, using wood trim, mitering one side, or by rounding the edge of the flat tile with a grinder. To avoid problems with the installation, you should always investigate the availability of trim tiles before finalizing your selection of ceramic tile.

Cleaning and Maintenance

Cleaning methods for ceramic tile vary depending on the condition of the tile and the service demands of the installation. Sometimes the tile and grout only require wiping with warm water and a damp cloth, mop, or sponge. At other times, a neutral cleaner should be added to the warm water. These neutral cleaners can be purchased from your local tile or grocery store. Generally, acid cleaners should not be used, since they can sometimes etch the surface of the tile. Still, vinegar can work well for some types of glazed tile. Nor should soap be used, since it leaves a dull film on the surface of the tile. It is always best to use a neutral cleaner and to schedule cleaning procedures at regular intervals to prevent a build-up of dirt or stains. When in doubt, consult the tile manufacturer for recommendations for cleaning.

Grouts sometimes require additional attention, since they are usually slightly recessed and tend to hold surface dirt and stains. Gentle scrubbing with a bristle brush and neutral cleaner will ensure that the grout is thoroughly cleaned. In some cases, grout that is very dirty, cracked, or powdery must be removed and replaced with new grout. Or it may be desirable to paint the grout lines with a grout stain to cover the stain and create a clean, new look.

The cleanability and stain resistance of some unglazed tiles and cementicious grouts can be improved with the application of sealers. This solution is especially effective for installations where food and grease spills are likely. Sealers are available in two varieties—penetrating sealers and topical or surface sealers.

Penetrating sealers are subsurface sealers that fill the microscopic pores in tile and grout. They work most effectively on the more porous types of tile classified as semivitreous or nonvitreous. Because very dense tiles may not accept penetrating sealers, always consult the tile manufacturer.

Topical or surface sealers are also available for use on unglazed tile. These products give a shiny appearance and provide stain resistance but actually increase maintenance, since they must be periodically stripped and reapplied. Soft-bodied, unglazed tiles often require the use of a topical sealer to increase the durability of the tile. Some terra cotta tiles are so soft that the topical sealer is required to keep the tile from wearing away. Because application of topical sealers is not always successful, you should always perform a test on extra, loose tiles or in an inconspicuous part of the floor. Scratching, discoloration, and wear patterns are potential problems with topical sealers.

Directory

Architects and Designers

de Falla & Dawson
Interior Spaces Planning and Design
1235 Linda Ridge Road
Pasadena, California 91103
(818) 793-2406

Enos & Company
705 North Alfred
Los Angeles, California 90069
(213) 655-0109

Jane Woulfe, A.S.I.D. Interior Design
942 Santa Hidalga
Solana Beach, California 92075
(619) 755-3463

Marieann Green, I.S.I.D.
Interior Design
8721 Santa Monica Blvd.
Los Angeles, California 90069
(310) 854-0605

Maude MacGillivray Incorporated
309 South Orlando Avenue
Los Angeles, California 90048
(213) 651-4395

MC Brandt Interior Design
Box 8276
La Jolla, California 92038
(619) 454-4300

Morse Ltd.
Paul Morse, A.S.I.D.
Certified Interior Designer
4413 Antigua Way
Oxnard, California 93035
(805) 985-0281

Penza Baukhages Architects
2203 N. Charles Street
Baltimore, MD 21218
(410) 467-7741

Ruth Livingston Interior Design
74 Main Street
Tiburon, California 94920
(415) 435-5264

Swann/Hall Associates Ltd.
857 Park Avenue
Baltimore, Maryland 21201
(410) 576-8780

Installation Materials

Mapei
1350 Lively Boulevard
Elk Grove Village, Illinois 60007
(708) 364-4470

Photographers

Laurie Black Photographer
22085 Salamo Road
West Linn, Oregon 97068
(503) 655-5939

Phillip H. Ennis Photography
98 Smith Street
Freeport, New York 11520
(516) 379-4273

Ann Gummerson
811 South Ann
Baltimore, Maryland 21231
(410) 276-6936

Norman McGrath Photographer
164 West 79th Street
New York, New York 10024
(212) 799-6422

Roger Miller Photo, Ltd.
1411 Hollins Street/Union Square
Baltimore, Maryland 21223
(410) 566-1222

Tile Companies

A Mano
Handmade Ceramic Tile
P.O. Box B
Camp Meeker, California 95419
(707) 874-2538

Alison Cooper Tile
P.O. Box 3095
Manhattan Beach, California 90266
(310) 546-9001

American Marazzi Tile
359 Clay Road
Sunnyvale, Texas 75182-9710
(214) 226-0110

American Olean Tile Company
1000 Cannon Avenue
Lansdale, Pennsylvania 19446-0271
(215) 393-2237

Ann Sacks Tile & Stone
1355 Market Street
Suite 104
San Francisco, California 94103
(415) 252-5889

Architectural Accents
5353 W. Sopris Creek Rd.
Basalt, Colorado 81621
(303) 927-3056

Benedikt Strebel Ceramics
978 Guerrero Street
San Francisco, California 94110
(415) 824-7949

Buchtal Corporation USA
1325 Northmeadow Parkway
Suite 114
Roswell, Georgia 30076
(404) 442-5500

Buena Tile
1717 Palma Drive
Ventura, California 93003
(805) 647-9233

Carla Funk, Ceramic Tile Artist
426 Village Run East
Encinitas, California 92024
(619) 943-7058

Cedit, S.P.A.
Via Vallassina, 21
22040 Lurago D'Erba Como Italy
Tel. 031/699051
Fax 031/699441

Ceramic Tile Trends
3251 Oradell Lane
Dallas, Texas 75220
(214) 358-5557

Ceramiche Caesar S.P.A.
Via Canaletto, 49
41040 Spezzano di Fiorano (MO) Italy
Tel. 0536/817111
Fax 0536/843540

Ceramitex, Inc.
Matthews Building West
312 W. Main Street
Suite 3W
Owosso, Michigan 48867
(517) 723-3859

Cheyne Walk, Inc.
327 Hernando Avenue
Sarasota, Florida 34243
(813) 355-3404

Christine Belfor Design, Ltd.
Art on Ceramic Tile
177 East 87th Street
Studio 402
New York, New York 10128
(212) 722-5410

Country Floors, Inc.
15 East 16th Street
New York, New York 10003
(212) 627-8300

Crossville Ceramics
P.O. Box 1168
Crossville, Tennessee 38557
(615) 484-2110

Dal-Tile Corporation
7834 Hawn Freeway
Dallas, Texas 75217
(800) 527-1249
Texas (800) 442-0418

Deborah Hecht Custom Design on Tile
1865 Harvest Lane
Bloomfield Hills, Michigan 48302
(810) 333-2168

Designs in Tile
Box 358—Department D
Mount Shasta, California 96067
(916) 926-2629

Dodge Tile
3528 Bagley Avenue N.
Seattle, Washington 98103
(206) 545-6900

Dunis Studios
2469 Hiline Drive
Bulverde, Texas 78163
(210) 438-7715

Ellie Hudovernik, Tilemaker
P.O. Box 49
Cascade, Wisconsin 53011
(414) 564-2913

Elon, Inc.
5 Skyline Drive
Hawthorne, New York 10532
(914) 347-7800

Epro, Inc.
156 East Broadway
Westerville, Ohio 43081
(614) 882-6990

Firebird, Inc.
335 Snyder Avenue
Berkeley Heights, New Jersey 07922
(908) 464-4613

Florida Tile Industries
P.O. Box 447
Lakeland, Florida 33802
(813) 687-7171

Brian C. Flynn and Associates
8687 Melrose Avenue, B447
Los Angeles, California 90069
(310) 659-2614

Florim Ceramiche, S.P.A.
Via Canaletto n. 24
41042 Fiorano (Modena) Italy
C.F. e P IVA 01265320364

Giorgini Design
Route 67, Box 126
Freehold, New York 12431
(518) 634-2559

H & R Johnson Tiles, Ltd.
Highgate Tile Works
Tunstall
Stoke-on-Trent
ST6 4JX England
Tel. 0782/575575
Fax 0782/577377

Hastings Tile & Il Bagno Collection
30 Commercial Street
Freeport, New York 11520
(516) 379-3500

Interceramic, USA
1624 W. Crosby Road
Suite 120
Carrollton, Texas 75006
(800) 365-6733

Jensen/Marineau Tile
22017 N.W. Beck
Portland, Oregon 97231
(503) 621-3487

La Maison Française
8435 Melrose Avenue
Los Angeles, California 90069
(213) 653-6534

Latco Products
2943 Gleneden Street
Los Angeles, California 90039
(213) 664-1171

Malibu Ceramics
P.O. Box 1406
Topanga, California 90290
(818) 700-5191

McIntyre Tile Company, Inc.
55 W. Grant Street
Post Office Box 14
Healdsburg, California 95448
(707) 433-8866

Metropolitan Ceramics
P.O. Box 9240
Canton, Ohio 44711-9240
(216) 484-4876

Monarch Tile, Inc.
P.O. Box 999
Florence, Alabama 35631
(205) 764-6181

Motawi Tileworks
3301 Packard
Ann Arbor, Michigan 48108
(313) 971-0765

Native Tile & Ceramics
4230 Glencoe Avenue
Marina Del Rey, California 90292
(310) 823-8684

New Image Tile
P.O. Box 139
Mt. Freedom, New Jersey 07970
(201) 328-4604

Peace Valley Tile
64 Beulah Road
New Britain, Pennsylvania 18901
(215) 340-0888

Peter King/Marni Jaime
Stonehaus
2617 N. 12th Avenue
Pensacola, Florida 32503
(904) 438-3273

Pewabic Pottery
10125 East Jefferson Avenue
Detroit, Michigan 48214
(313) 822-0954

Porcelanosa Ceramica
Carretera N-340, Km. 56,2
12540 Villarreal
Castellon, Spain
Tel. 3464/521262
Fax 3464/527258

Pratt & Larsen Tile
1201 S.E. Third Avenue
Portland, Oregon 97214
(503) 231-9464

Pull Cart Tiles, Inc.
31 West 21st Street
7th floor
New York, New York 10010
(212) 727-7089

Quarry Tile Company
Building 12, Spokane Industrial Park
Spokane, Washington 99216
(509) 924-1466

Renato Bisazza, Inc.
8032 N.W. 66th Street
Miami, Florida 33166
(305) 597-4099

Rhein Lockwood Studios
551 Thomas Street
Stroudsburg, Pennsylvania 18360
(717) 424-1980

Rhombold Sax
8904 Beverly Blvd.
West Hollywood, California
(310) 550-0170

Dennis Ruabon, Ltd.
Hafod Tileries, Ruabon
Wrexham, Clwyd, LL14 6ET
North Wales, Great Britian
Tel. 0978/843484
Fax 0978/843276

Santex Ceramiche D'Arte
Via Regina Pacis Nr. 214
41049 Sassuolo, MO, Italy
Tel. 0536/800133
Fax 0536/802482

Starbuck Goldner Tile
315 W. Fourth Street
Bethlehem, Pennsylvania 18015
(215) 866-6321

Stellar Ceramics, Inc.
55 West Grant Street
Healdsburg, California 95448
(707) 433-8166

Summitville Tiles, Inc.
Summitville, Ohio 43962
(216) 223-1511

Sunny McLean & Company
3800 N.E. 40th Street
Miami, Florida 33137
(305) 573-5943

The Meredith Collection
P.O. Box 8854
Canton, Ohio 44711
(216) 484-1656

The Tileworks
4140 Grand Avenue
Des Moines, Iowa 50312
(515) 255-1300

TileCera, Inc.
300 Arcata Blvd.
Clarksville, Tennessee 37040
(615) 645-5100

Walker Zanger
8901 Bradley Avenue
Sun Valley, California 91352
(818) 504-0235

Wirth/Salander Studios
132 Washington Street
South Norwalk, Connecticut 06854
(203) 852-9449

Tile Manufacturing Equipment Suppliers

Harrop Industries, Inc.
3470 East Fifth Avenue
Columbus, Ohio 43219-1797
(614) 231-3621

Trade Associations

American National Standards Institute
1430 Broadway
New York, New York 10018
(212) 354-3300

American Society for Testing and Materials
1916 Race Street
Philadelphia, Pennsylvania 19103
(215) 299-5400

National Tile Contractors Association, Inc.
P.O. Box 13629
Jackson, Mississippi 39236
(601) 939-2071

Ceramic Tile Distributors Association
800 Roosevelt Road
Building C, Suite 20
Glen Ellyn, Illinois 60137
(708) 545-9415

Italian Tile Center
499 Park Avenue
New York, New York 10022
(212) 980-1500

Materials and Methods Standards Association
P.O. Box 350
Grand Haven, Michigan 49417
(616) 842-7844

Tile Council of America
P.O. Box 326
Princeton, New Jersey 08542
(609) 921-7050

Tile Heritage Foundation
P.O. Box 1850
Healdsburg, California 95448
(707) 431-TILE

Tile Promotion Board
900 East Indiantown Road
Suite 211
Jupiter, Florida 33477
(407) 743-3150

Trade Commission of Spain
2655 LeJeune Road
Suite 1114
Coral Gables, Florida 33134
(305) 446-4387

Appendices

1. Ceramic Tile Industry Standards and Guides

Industry Standards

1. *American National Standard Specifications for Ceramic Tile—ANSI A137.1*

2. *American National Standard Specifications for the Installation of Ceramic Tile—ANSI A108 series*

3. *American National Standard Specifications for Ceramic Tile Installation Materials—ANSI A118 series and A136.1*

4. *American Society for Testing and Materials Standards*

Industry Guides

1. Tile Council of America's *Handbook for Ceramic Tile Installation*

2. *National Tile Contractors Association Reference Manual*

2. Floor Tile Performance Level Requirements

Performance Level	Primary Applications	Tile Requirement
Extra heavy	Industrial buildings such as food plants, dairies, and breweries	Quarry tile or packing house tile
Heavy	Heavy commercial use buildings such as shopping malls, stores, commercial kitchens, auto showrooms, and service areas	Quarry tile, paver tile, and—in some cases—ceramic mosaics
Moderate	Normal commercial and light institutional use in public spaces such as restaurants and hospitals	Ceramic mosaics or heavier tiles such as quarry tile and paver tile
Light	Light commercial use in office space, reception areas, kitchens, and bathrooms	Ceramic mosaics or heavier tiles such as quarry tile and paver tile
Residential	Residential kitchens, bathrooms, and foyers	Ceramic mosaics or heavier tiles such as quarry tile and paver tile

NOTE: Chart extrapolated from the Floor Tiling Installation Guide in the TCA's *Handbook for Ceramic Tile Installation*.

3. Water Absorption of Ceramic Tile
(as defined by ANSI A137.1)

Water Absorption	Types of Tile	Primary Application
0.5% or less	Impervious	Interiors and exteriors*
>0.5%–3.0%	Vitreous	Interiors and exteriors*
>3.0%–7.0%	Semivitreous	Interiors only*
>7.0%	Nonvitreous	Interiors only*

*These are general guidelines only. Always follow the manufacturer's recommendations for use, especially when installing tile outdoors in climates subject to freeze-thaw cycles.

4. Common Test Methods

The following is a brief description of the most common ceramic tile test methods and the significance of the procedure.

Tests developed by the American Society for Testing and Materials

ASTM C 373   *Standard Test Method for Water Absorption, Bulk Density, Apparent Porosity, and Apparent Specific Gravity of Fired Whiteware Products*
A test to determine the water absorption of ceramic tile by measuring the mass of the tile when dry and wet. This test measures the amount of moisture that can be absorbed into the tile.

ASTM C 424   *Standard Test Method for Crazing Resistance of Fired Glazed Whitewares by Autoclave Treatment*
A test to determine the crazing resistance of ceramic tile by subjecting the tile to increasing levels of pressure. An average failure pressure is assigned to the tile based on the amount of pressure required to cause failure.

ASTM C 482   *Standard Test Method for Bond Strength of Ceramic Tile to Portland Cement*
A test to determine the bond strength of ceramic tile to portland cement. Tile is bonded to a pure cement bond coat over a cement mortar bed then load is applied to the edge of the tile until failure occurs.

ASTM C 484   *Standard Test Method for Thermal Shock Resistance of Glazed Ceramic Tile*
A test to determine the resistance of glazed ceramic tile to five cycles of thermal shock. Tiles are heated in an oven to 293° F then quickly removed and placed on a sheet of aluminum.

ASTM C 485   *Standard Test Method for Measuring Warpage of Ceramic Tile*
A test to determine the warpage of ceramic tile by measuring the diagonal and edge curvatures and determining the deviation from a straight line. Excessive warpage can create unsatisfactory tile installations.

ASTM C 499   *Standard Test Method for Facial Dimensions and Thickness of Flat, Rectangular Ceramic Wall, and Floor Tile*
A test to determine the variations in length, width, and thickness of ceramic tile. Excessive variations in these dimensions can cause difficulties in installing tile.

ASTM C 501   *Standard Test Method for Relative Resistance to Wear of Unglazed Ceramic Tile by the Taber Abraser*
A test to determine the wearability of unglazed tiles using

an abrading machine. An abrasive wear index is assigned based on the loss of weight of the tile resulting from the abrading process. This test speaks to the durability of unglazed tiles.

ASTM C 502 *Standard Test Method for Wedging of Flat, Rectangular Ceramic Wall and Floor Tile*
A test to determine the percentage of wedging or out-of-squareness of a ceramic tile by measuring the length and width of opposite sides of the tile. Excessive wedging can cause difficulties in installing tile.

ASTM C 609 *Standard Test Method for Measurement of Small Color Differences Between Ceramic Wall or Floor Tile*
A test to determine small color differences between two pieces of solid-colored ceramic tile. This test speaks to the uniformity of the color of the glazed or unglazed tile.

ASTM C 648 *Standard Test Method for Breaking Strength of Ceramic Tile*
A test to determine the average breaking strength by applying load to ceramic tile until failure occurs.

ASTM C 1026 *Standard Test Method for Measuring the Resistance of Ceramic Tile to Freeze-Thaw Cycling*
A test to determine the resistance of ceramic tile to freeze/thaw cycles. Tiles are subjected to up to 15 cycles of freeze/thaw conditions and the number of damaged tiles with crazing, chipping, spalling, and cracks are reported.

ASTM C 1027 *Standard Test Method for Determining Visible Abrasion Resistance of Glazed Ceramic Tile*
A test to determine the visible abrasion resistance of glazed ceramic tile using steel balls in an abrading machine. A rating system known as the Abrasive Wear Index for Glazed Floor Tile was developed from this test. It assigns a rating scale of 1 to 4+ based on the visible abrasion of the tile. Glazes that show visible wear at 150 revolutions or less have a classification of 1. Glazes that do not show visible wear at 12,000 revolutions are classified at 4+. Tiles rated at 4+ must also pass a stain resistance test.

ASTM C 1028 *Standard Test Method for Evaluating the Static Coefficient of Friction of Ceramic Tile and Other Like Surfaces by the Horizontal Dynamometer Pull Meter Method*
A test to determine the static coefficient of friction of ceramic tile in both wet and dry conditions by pulling neo-

lite across the surface of the tile with a dynamometer pull meter. Twelve dry pulls and twelve wet pulls are made and an average static coefficient of friction is determined for both conditions.

Other Tests

Moh's Scale of Hardness

A set of values that may be used to determine the relative hardness of glazes by pulling minerals across the surface of the glaze and observing evidence of scratching. A rating scale of 1 to 10 is used, based on which mineral scratched the tile. The minerals are as follows:

1. talc
2. gypsum
3. calcite
4. fluorite
5. apatite
6. microcline
7. quartz
8. topaz
9. corundum
10. diamond

Abrasive Wear Index for Glazed Floor Tiles

See definition for ASTM C 1027.

Glossary

Unless otherwise noted, the following terms are included courtesy of the National Tile Contractors Association.

Abrasion Resistance: The ability of a tile surface to resist being worn by rubbing and friction. (Author's definition)

Abrasive Wear Index for Glazed Floor Tile: A rating system utilizing ASTM C1027 that determines the abrasion resistance of glazed ceramic tile on a scale of 1 to 4+. Glazes that show visible wear at 150 revolutions or less have a classification of 1. Glazes that do not show visible wear at 12,000 revolutions are classified at 4+. Tile rated at 4+ must also pass a stain resistance test. (Author's definition)

Absorption: The relationship of the weight of the water absorbed to the weight of the dry specimen, expressed in percentages.

Adhesive: See *Organic Adhesive.*

Admixture: A material other than water, aggregates, and hydraulic cement, used as an ingredient of concrete or mortar, and which is added immediately before or during its mixing.

Aggregate: Granular material, such as sand, gravel, or crushed stone, used with a cementing medium to form a hydraulic-cement or mortar.

Back-Butter: The spreading of a bond coat to the backs of ceramic tile just before the tile is placed.

Base: One or more rows of tile installed above the floor. See *Cove.*

Bicottura: Method for producing tile by firing it twice (the first fire is for the body, the second is to fuse glazes or patterns in glaze onto the body). Usually, there are two glazes on the tile, first a non-transparent glaze on the body, then a transparent glaze on the surface.

Bisque: The refined mixture of clay, water, and additives that has been shaped into the body of a tile.

Body: The structural portion of a ceramic tile. This term also refers to the material or mixture from which the tile is made.

Bond: The adherence of one material to another.

Bond Coat: A material used between the back of the tile and the prepared surface. Suitable bond coats include pure portland cement, dry-set portland cement mortar, latex–portland cement mortar, organic adhesive, epoxy mortar, or adhesive.

Bond Strength: A bond coat's ability to resist separating from the tile and setting bed. Measured in pounds per square inch (psi).

Bullnose: A trim tile with a convex radius on one edge. This tile is used for finishing the top of a wainscot or for turning an outside corner.

Buttering: See *Back-Butter*.

Caulk: See *Sealant*.

Caulking compound: Waterproof caulking material. See *Sealant*.

Cement: Usually refers to portland cement that is mixed with sand, gravel, and water to form concrete.

Cement Grout: A cementitious mixture of portland cement, sand, or other ingredients and water, to produce a water-resistant, uniformly colored material used to fill the joints between the tile units.

Cementitious: Having the properties of cement.

Cementitious Backer Unit: See *Glass Mesh Mortar Unit*.

Ceramic Mosaic Tile: Tile formed by either the dust-pressed or plastic method, usually $^1/_4$ inch thick, and having a facial area of less than six square inches. Ceramic mosaic tiles may be of either porcelain or natural clay composition and they may be either plain or have an abrasive mixture throughout.

Ceramic Tile: See definition for *Tile*.

Cleavage Membrane: A membrane that provides a separation and slip sheet between the mortar setting bed and the backing or base surface.

Coefficient of Friction: A measure of the resistance to slipping that occurs when a pedestrian's footwear comes in contact with a ceramic tile surface.

Colored Grout: Commercially prepared grout consisting of carefully graded aggregate, portland cement, water dispersing agents, plasticizers, and colorfast pigments.

Commercial Portland Cement Grout: A mixture of portland cement with other ingredients to produce a water-resistant, dense, uniformly colored material.

Conventional Installation: See *Thick-Bed Mortar*.

Cove: A trim tile unit having one edge with a concave radius. A cove is used to form a junction between the bottom wall course and the floor or to form an inside corner.

Cove Base (Sanitary): A trim tile having a concave radius on one edge and a convex radius on the opposite edge. This base is used as the only course of tile above the floor tile.

Crazing: The cracking that occurs in fired glazes or other ceramic coatings due to critical tensile stresses (minute surface cracks).

Curing: Maintenance of humidity and temperature of the freshly placed mortar or grout during some definite period following the placing or finishing, to assure satisfactory hydration of portland cement and proper hardening of the mortar or grout.

Damp Curing: See *Curing*.

Deflection: A variation in the position or shape of a structure or structural element due to the effects of loads or volume change, usually measured as a linear deviation from an established plane rather than an angular variation.

Decorative Tile: Ceramic tile with a ceramic decoration on the surface.

Double-fired Tile: See *Bicottura*.

Dry-set Mortar: A mixture of portland cement with sand and additives imparting water retentivity that is used as a bond coat for setting tile. Normally, when this mortar is used, neither the tile nor walls have to be soaked during installation.

Dust-pressed tile: A tile unit that is formed by pressing clays that are ground and dried to a fine powder.

Dusting: The application of dry portland cement to a wet floor or deck mortar surface.

Elastomeric: Any of various elastic substances resembling rubber.

Embossed: A decoration in relief or excised on the wear surface of the tile.

Encaustic Tile: A decorative tile with carved designs filled with liquefied, colored clay.

Epoxy Adhesive: An adhesive system employing epoxy resin and epoxy hardener portions.

Epoxy Grout: A mortar system employing epoxy resin and epoxy hardener portions.

Epoxy Mortar: A system employing epoxy resins and hardener portions, often containing coarse silica filler, that is usually formulated for industrial and commercial installations where chemical resistance is of paramount importance.

Epoxy Resin: An epoxy composition used as a chemical resistant setting adhesive or chemical-resistant grout.

Expansion Joint: A joint through tile, mortar, and reinforcing wire down to the substrate.

Extruded Tile: A tile unit that is formed when plastic clay mixtures are forced through a pug mill opening (die) of suitable configuration, resulting in a continuous ribbon of formed clay. A wire cutter or similar cut-off device is then used to cut the ribbon into appropriate lengths and widths of tile.

Facial Defect: That portion of the tile's facial surface readily observed to be nonconforming and that detracts from the aesthetic appearance or serviceability of the installed tile.

Faience Tile: Glazed or unglazed tile, generally made by the plastic process with characteristic variations in the face, edges, and glaze. These variations produce a handcrafted, decorative effect.

Firing: The controlled heat treatment of ceramic tile in a kiln during the process of manufacture, to develop the desired properties.

Floor Tile: A ceramic tile, either glazed or unglazed, with physical properties making them suitable for use in pedestrian walkways.

Frost-proof Tile: Tile manufactured for use where freezing and thawing conditions occur.

Glass Mesh Mortar Unit: A backer board designed for use with ceramic tile in wet areas. It can be used in place of metal lath, portland cement scratch coat, and mortar bed.

Glass Mosaic Tiles: Tile made of glass, usually in sizes not over 2" sq. and $1/4$" thick, and mounted on sheets of paper. The sheets are usually 12" x 24".

Glaze: A ceramic coating matured to the glassy state on ceramic tile. The term glaze also refers to the material or mixture from which the coating is made.

Glazed Tile: Tile with a fused impervious facial finish composed of ceramic materials fused to the body of the tile, which may be nonvitreous, semi-vitreous, vitreous, or impervious.

Glazed Wall Tile: See *Wall Tile*.

Green Tile: An unfired bisque.

Grout: A cementitious or other type material used for filling joints between tile.

Impervious Tile: Tile with water absorption of 0.5 percent or less.

Kiln: An oven used to fire tile.

Latex–Portland Cement Grout: Combines portland cement grout with a special latex additive.

Latex–Portland Cement Mortar: A mixture of portland cement, sand, and a special latex additive used as a bond coat for setting ceramic tile.

Lath: Metal mesh which acts as a backing or reinforcing agent for the scratch coat or mortar.

Leveling Coat: See *Plumb Scratch*.

Lugs: Protuberances attached to tiles to maintain even spacing for grout lines.

Mastic: Tile adhesives. See *Organic Adhesive*.

Modified Epoxy Emulsion Mortar: A system employing epoxy resin and epoxy hardener with portland cement and sand. This material can be used as a mortar or grout, but it is not chemical resistant.

Moh's Scale of Hardness: A set of values that may be used to determine the relative hardness of glazes using minerals. The rating scale is 1 to 10.

Monocottura: Method of producing tile by a single firing. Tiles may be glazed or unglazed.

Mortar: A mixture of cement paste and fine aggregate: in fresh concrete, the material occupying the interstices among particles of coarse aggregate; in masonry construction, mortar may contain masonry cement, or may contain hydraulic cement with lime (and possibly other admixtures) to afford greater plasticity and workability than are attainable with standard hydraulic cement mortar. (*CT Manual*)

Mosaic Tile: See *Ceramic Mosaic Tile*.

Mud: A slang term for mortar.

Murals: Tile installed in a precise area of a wall or floor to provide a decorative design or picture. Glass or marble mosaic tile (tesserae) made to form a picture or design. Ceramic tile, painted and fired to form a picture or design.

Natural Clay Tile: A ceramic mosaic tile or a paver tile made by either the dust-pressed or the plastic method from clays which produce a dense body having a distinctive slightly textured appearance.

Neat Cement: Portland cement mixed with water to a desired creamy consistency. See *Pure Coat*.

Neolite: A common shoe and sole material.

Nominal Sizes: The approximate facial size or thickness of tile, expressed in inches or fractions of an inch.

Nonvitreous Tile: Tile with water absorption of more than 7.0 percent.

Notched Trowel: A trowel with a serrated or notched edge. It is used for the application of a gauged amount of tile mortar or adhesive in ridges of a specific thickness.

Organic Adhesive: A prepared organic material, ready to use with no further addition of liquid or powder, that cures or sets by evaporation.

Paver Tile: Glazed or unglazed porcelain or natural clay tile formed by the dust-pressed method having six square inches or more of facial area.

Physical Properties of Ceramic Tile: Those properties of tile as measured by the ASTM tests referred to in ANSI.

Plumb Scratch: An additional scratch coat that has been applied to obtain a uniform setting bed on a plumb vertical plane.

Porcelain Enamel Institute Rating: See *Abrasive Wear Index for Glazed Floor Tile*.

Porcelain Tile: A ceramic mosaic tile or paver tile generally made by the dust-pressed method from a composition that results in a tile that is dense, impervious, fine-grained, and smooth, with sharply formed face.

Portland Cement: A manufactured hydraulic cement composed of lime, silica, iron oxide, and alumina.

Pure Coat: Neat cement applied to the mortar bed.

Quarry Tile: Glazed or unglazed tile, made by the extrusion process from natural clay or shale, usually having 6" sq. or more of facial area.

Rubber Trowel: The rubber trowel used for grouting. A nonporous synthetic-rubber-faced float that is mounted on an aluminum back with a wood handle. This trowel is used to force material into tile joints, remove excess grout, and form a smooth grout finish.

Saltillo Tile: A type of terra cotta tile that is handmade, nonvitreous, and composed of natural clay from the region surrounding Saltillo, Mexico. The clay is blended with water, molded, dried, and fired at low temperatures. See *Terra Cotta Tile*. (Author's definition)

Scratch Coat: A mixture of portland cement, sand, and water applied as the first coat of mortar on a wall or ceiling. Its surface usually is scratched or roughened so that it will bond properly with subsequent coats of mortar.

Sealant: An elastomeric material used to fill and seal expansion and control joints. This material prevents the passage of moisture and allows horizontal and lateral movement at the expansion and control joints.

Self-spacing Tile: Tile with lugs, spacers, or protuberances on the sides that automatically space the tile for the grout joints.

Semivitreous Tile: Tile with water absorption of more than 3.0 percent, but not more than 7.0 percent.

Setting Bed: The layer of mortar on which the tile is set. The final coat of mortar on a wall or ceiling also may be called a setting bed.

Silicone Grout: An engineered elastomeric grout system for interior use.

Single-fired Tile: See *Monocottura*.

Slip-resistant Tile: Tile having slip-resistant characteristics due to an abrasive admixture, abrasive particles in the surface, or grooves or patterns in the surface.

Slurry Coat: A mixture of pure portland cement and water to a trowelable consistency. (TCA)

Spacers: Plastic, rubber, wood, or rope used in wall or floor installations to separate tiles. Manufactured spacers are available in thicknesses from $1/16$" to $1/2$".

Standard-Grade Ceramic Tile: Highest grade of all types of ceramic tile.

Subfloor: A rough floor—plywood or boards—laid over joists and on which an underlayment or substrate is installed.

Substrate: The underlying support for ceramic tile installations.

Terra Cotta Tile: A fired natural-clay tile, of variable color, ranging from red to red-yellow in hue. It may be either machinemade or handmade.

Thick-bed Mortar: A thick layer of mortar (more than $1/2$") that is used for leveling. Also known as a conventional installation.

Thin-set: The term used to describe the installation of tile with all materials except portland cement mortar, which is the only recognized thick-bed method.

Tile: A ceramic surfacing unit, usually relatively thin in relation to facial area, made from clay or a mixture of clay and other ceramic materials called the body of the tile, having either a glazed or unglazed face. Fired at a temperature sufficiently high to produce specific physical properties and characteristics.

Tile Cutter: Special machine to cut ceramic tile.

Tile Nipper: Special pliers that nibble away little bites of ceramic tile to create small, irregular, or curved cuts.

Trim Tiles: Tiles of various shapes consisting of such items as bases, caps, corners, moldings, and angles, necessary to achieve installations of the desired architectural design.

Unglazed Tile: A hard, dense tile of uniform composition throughout, deriving color and texture from the materials of which the body is made.

Vitreous Tile: Tile with water absorption of more than 0.5 percent, but not more than 3.0 percent.

Wall Tile: A glazed tile with a body that is suitable for interior use and that is usually nonvitreous, and is not required nor expected to withstand excessive impact or be subject to freezing and thawing conditions.

Waterproof Membrane: A covering applied to a substrate before tiling to protect the substrate and framing from damage by water. May be applied below mortar beds or directly beneath thin-set tiles.

Bibliography

Alexander, Christopher, *The Timeless Way of Building* (Oxford University Press, New York, NY, 1979).

National Tile Contractors Association Technical Committee, *National Tile Contractors Association Reference Manual*, 2d ed. (National Tile Contractors Association, Jackson, MS, 1989).

Tile Council of America, *American National Standard Specifications for Ceramic Tile—ANSI A137.1* (Tile Council of America, Princeton, NJ, 1992).

Tile Council of America, *American National Standard Specifications for the Installation of Ceramic Tile—ANSI A108 series* (Tile Council of America, Princeton, NJ, 1992).

Tile Council of America, *American National Standard Specifications for Installation Materials for Ceramic Tile—ANSI A118 series and A136.1* (Tile Council of America, Princeton, NJ, 1992).

Tile Council of America, *1994 Handbook for Ceramic Tile Installation* (Tile Council of America, Princeton, NJ, 1994).

Index

Page numbers in *italics* refer to illustrations and captions.

Supplier and Photography Credits

Front Cover. Photo courtesy Deborah Hecht Custom Design on Tile. Tile: Deborah Hecht Custom Design on Tile. Photographer: Deborah Hecht

Front Cover Flap, item 1. Photo courtesy Ellie Hudovernik. Tile: Ellie Hudovernik, Tilemaker

Front Cover Flap, item 2. Photo courtesy Dale Wiley. Tile: A Mano

Front Cover Flap, item 3. Photo courtesy Motawi Tileworks. Tile: Motawi Tileworks

Front Cover Flap, item 4. Photo courtesy Ceramic Tile Trends. Tile: Ceramic Tile Trends

Back Cover. Photo courtesy Hastings Tile. Tile: Italian ceramic tile by Vogue and Gabbianelli from Hastings Tile. Designer: Barbara Ostrom. Photographer: Phillip H. Ennis

Back Cover Flap. Photographer: Amy Jones Photographer

Page ii. Photo courtesy Hastings Tile. Tile: Italian ceramic tile by Vogue and Gabbianelli from Hastings Tile. Designer: Barbara Ostrom. Photographer: Phillip H. Ennis

Page v. Photo courtesy Jeffrey Penza. Tile: Hastings Tile. Architect: Penza Baukhages Architects. Interior Designer: Swann/Hall Associates. Photographer: Ann Gummerson

Page vi. Photo courtesy Deborah Hecht Custom Design on Tile. Tile: Deborah Hecht Custom Design on Tile. Photographer: Deborah Hecht

Page viii. Photo courtesy Cedit S.P.A. Tile: Cedit S.P.A.

Page x. Photo courtesy Pratt & Larsen Tile. Tile: Pratt & Larsen Tile. Designer: Lucinda Parker. Photographer: Laurie Black Photography

Page 1. Photo courtesy Florida Tile Industries. Tile: Florida Tile

Page 4. Photo courtesy Trade Commission of Spain. Tile: Tile of Spain

Page 7, item 2. Photo courtesy H & R Johnson Tiles, Ltd. Tile: H & R Johnson

Page 7, item 3. Photo courtesy H & R Johnson Tiles, Ltd. Tile: H & R Johnson

Page 9. Photo courtesy TileCera, Inc.

Page 11. Photo courtesy TileCera, Inc.

Page 12. Photo courtesy TileCera, Inc.

Page 13. Photo courtesy TileCera, Inc.

Page 14, item 8. Photo courtesy Stellar Ceramics, Inc.

Page 14, item 9. Photo courtesy Stellar Ceramics, Inc.

Page 15. Photo courtesy Stellar Ceramics, Inc.

Page 16. Photo courtesy Stellar Ceramics, Inc.

Page 17. Photo courtesy Mary Clare Brandt, A.S.I.D. Tile: Latco Products distributed through Finest City Ceramics. Designer: Mary Clare Brandt, A.S.I.D. Photographer: Eugene Tapp

Page 19, item 13. Photo courtesy American Olean Tile Company. Tile: American Olean

Page 19, item 14. Photo courtesy American Olean Tile Company. Tile: American Olean

Page 20. Photo courtesy New Image Tile. Tile: New Image Tile. Designer: Peg Kesmodel of Swann/Hall Associates, Ltd. Photographer: Ann Gummerson

Page 21. Photo courtesy New Image Tile. Tile: New Image Tile. Designer: Peg Kesmodel of Swann/Hall Associates, Ltd. Photographer: Ann Gummerson

Page 22. Photo courtesy Peter King and Marni Jaime. Tile: Peter King and Marni Jaime

Page 22. Drawing courtesy Summitville Tiles, Inc.

Page 23, item 19. Photo courtesy Ceramiche Caesar. Tile: Ceramiche Caesar

Page 23, item 20. Photo courtesy Trade Commission of Spain. Tile: Tile of Spain

Page 25. Photo courtesy Summitville Tiles, Inc. Tile: Summitville Tiles, Inc.

Page 26. Photo courtesy Buchtal Ceramics. Tile: Buchtal Ceramics

Page 27. Photo courtesy American Olean Tile Company. Tile: American Olean

Page 29. Photo courtesy Metropolitan Ceramics. Tile: Metropolitan Ceramics

Page 30. Photo courtesy American Olean Tile Company. Tile: American Olean

Page 32. Photo courtesy Trade Commission of Spain. Tile: Tile of Spain

Page 33. Photo courtesy Renato Bisazza. Tile: Bisazza Mosaico

Page 34, item 37. Photo courtesy Selene Seltzer. Tile: Designs in Tile

Page 34, item 38. Photo courtesy Kathleen Rhein Lockwood. Tile: Rhein Lockwood Studios

Page 34, item 39. Photo courtesy Santex Ceramiche D'Arte. Tile: Santex Ceramiche D'Arte

Page 34, item 40. Photo courtesy Frank Giorgini. Tile: Giorgini Design. Photographer: DeBora Goletz

Page 35, item 41. Photo courtesy Motawi Tileworks. Tile: Motawi Tileworks

Page 35, item 42. Photo courtesy Dale Wiley. Tile: A Mano

Page 35, item 43. Photo courtesy Ellie Hudovernik. Tile: Ellie Hudovernik, Tilemaker

Page 35, item 44. Photo courtesy Ursula Dodge. Tile: Dodge Tile

Page 36. Photo courtesy Firebird, Inc. Tile: Firebird, Inc. Photographer: Technifinish

Pages 44 and 45. Photo courtesy Florida Tile Industries. Tile: Florida Tile

Page 47. Photo courtesy Mark Enos. Tile: Brian C. Flynn and Associates. Designer: Enos & Company

Page 48. Photo courtesy Wirth/Salander Studios. Tile and ceramic framed mirror: Wirth/Salander Studios. Designer: Kolaski Associates, Inc. Photographer: Kurt Dolnier

Page 49. Photo courtesy Ceramic Tile Trends. Tile: Ceramic Tile Trends

Page 50. Photo courtesy Walker Zanger Tile. Tile: McIntyre Tile available through Walker Zanger Tile. Photographer: Larry Renolds

Page 51. Photo courtesy Crossville Ceramics. Tile: Crossville Ceramics

Page 52. Photo courtesy Florim Ceramiche, S.P.A. Tile: Floor Gres

Page 53. Photo courtesy The Meredith Collection. Tile: The Meredith Collection

Page 54, item 55. Photo courtesy H & R Johnson Tiles, Ltd. Tile: Minton Hollins by H & R Johnson

Page 54, item 56. Photo courtesy Carla Funk. Tile: Carla Funk Ceramic Tile Artist

Page 55. Photo courtesy Buchtal Ceramics. Tile: Buchtal Ceramics

Page 57. Photo courtesy Hastings Tile. Tile: Italian ceramic tile from Hastings Tile. Designer: Barbara Ostrom. Photographer: Phillip H. Ennis

Page 60. Photo courtesy Trade Commission of Spain. Tile: Tile of Spain

Page 61. Photo courtesy Benedikt Strebel. Tile: Benedikt Strebel. Photographer: Muffy Kibbey

Page 62. Photo courtesy Elon Tile. Tile: Elon Tile

Page 63. Photo courtesy Christine Belfor Design, Ltd. Tile: Christine Belfor Design. Photographer: Ted Belfor

Page 65. Photo courtesy The Tileworks. Tile: The Tileworks

Page 67. Photo courtesy Latco Products. Tile: Latco Products. Designers: Paul Morse and Jone Pence. Photographer: Peter Malinowski

Page 68. Photo courtesy Florim Ceramiche, S.P.A. Tile: Floor Gres

Page 70. Photo courtesy Dal-Tile Corporation. Tile: Dal-Tile. Designer: James and Cheryl Hughes. Tile Contractor: Abstract Marble & Tile

Page 71, item 72. Photo courtesy Peace Valley Tile. Tile: Peace Valley Tile

Page 71, item 73. Photo courtesy Cheyne Walk, Inc. by permission Ginny Gater. Tile: Cheyne Walk

Page 72. Photo courtesy The Meredith Collection. Tile: The Meredith Collection

Page 75. Photo courtesy Ruth Livingston Interior Design. Tile: Ann Sacks Tile & Stone. Designer: Ruth Livingston Interior Design. Photographer: John Vaughan

Page 76. Photo courtesy McIntyre Tile. Tile: McIntyre Tile

Page 77. Photo courtesy Dale Wiley. Tile: A Mano

Pages 78 and 79. Photo courtesy Florida Tile Industries. Tile: Florida Tile

Page 81. Photo courtesy Interceramic, USA. Tile: Interceramic

Page 83. Photo courtesy Jane Woulfe, A.S.I.D. Tile: Latco Products. Designer: Jane Woulfe, A.S.I.D.

Page 84. Photo courtesy Pull Cart Tiles, Inc. Tile: Pull Cart Tiles. Photographer: David F. Mansure

Page 85. Photo courtesy Sunny McLean & Company. Residence: Dennis Jenkins and Sunny McLean. Tile: Stained Glass Unlimited. Mosaic design: Kim Rizio. Photographer: Dan Forer

Page 86. Photo courtesy Benedikt Strebel. Tile: Benedikt Strebel. Photographer: Richard Ross

Page 87. Photo courtesy Italian Tile Center. Tile: Italian ceramic tile by Imola. Designer: Anne Marie Baldine

Page 89, item 85. Photo courtesy Country Floors. Tile: Country Floors

Page 89, item 86. Photo courtesy Country Floors. Tile: Country Floors

Page 91. Photo courtesy Florim Ceramiche, S.P.A. Tile: Floor Gres

Page 93. Photos courtesy Marieann Green, I.S.I.D. Tile: La Maison Francaise. Designer: Marieann Green, I.S.I.D.

Page 94. Photo courtesy Hastings Tile. Tile: Italian ceramic tile by Imola from Hastings Tile. Designer: Barbara Ostrom

Page 95. Tile: Country Floors. Photographer: Phillip Ennis

Page 97. Tile: Italian ceramic tile from Hastings Tile. Designer: Stewart Skolnick. Photographer: Norman McGrath

Page 98. Photo courtesy Malibu Ceramics. Tile: Malibu Ceramics. Photographer: Grant Mudford

Page 99. Photo courtesy Malibu Ceramics. Tile: Malibu Ceramics. Photographer: Grant Mudford

Page 100. Photo courtesy de Falla & Dawson. Tile: Porcelanosa. Designer: de Falla & Dawson Interior Spaces, Planning & Design

Page 101. Photo courtesy de Falla & Dawson. Tile: Porcelanosa. Designer: de Falla & Dawson Interior Spaces, Planning & Design

Page 102. Photo courtesy Maude MacGillivray, A.S.I.D. Tile: Rhombold Sax. Architect: T. Scott MacGillivray, A.I.A. Interior Designer: Maude MacGillivray, A.S.I.D.

Page 103. Photo courtesy Maude MacGillivray, A.S.I.D. Tile: Rhombold Sax. Architect: T. Scott MacGillivray, A.I.A. Interior Designer: Maude MacGillivray, A.S.I.D.

Pages 104 and 105. Photo courtesy Florida Tile Industries. Tile: Florida Tile

Page 107. Photo courtesy Paul Morse. Countertop tile: Latco Products. Floor tile: Buena Tile. Designers: Paul Morse, Jone Pence, Elizabeth Alexander, and Judy Ellis. Photographer: Bentley/Terrill

Page 110. Tile: Italian ceramic tile by Sicis from Hastings Tile. Designer: Gail Green. Photographer: Phillip Ennis

Page 112. Photo courtesy Latco Products. Tile: Latco Products

Page 114. Photo courtesy Wirth/Salander Studios. Tile: Wirth/Salander Studios. Designer: Barbara Mintz. Photographer: Christine Rose

Page 115. Photo courtesy Wirth/Salander Studios. Tile: Wirth/Salander Studios. Designer: Barbara Mintz. Photographer: Christine Rose

Pages 116 and 117. Photo courtesy Florida Tile Industries. Tile: Florida Tile

Page 120. Photo courtesy Hastings Tile. Tile: Glass mosaic from Hastings Tile. Designer: Ted Karagannis

Page 121. Photo courtesy Hastings Tile. Tile: Glass mosaic from Hastings Tile. Designer: Ted Karagannis

Page 123. Photo courtesy Hastings Tile. Tile: Italian ceramic tile by Grazia from Hastings Tile. Designer: Dennis Rolland

Page 124. Photo courtesy Hastings Tile. Tile: Italian ceramic tile by Grazia from Hastings Tile. Designer: Dennis Rolland

Page 126. Photo courtesy Stellar Ceramics. Tile: Stellar Ceramics available through Mission Tile West Showroom in South Pasadena, California

Page 128. Photo courtesy Barbara Jensen. Tile: Jensen/Marineau Tile available through Country Floors

Page 129. Photo courtesy Barbara Jensen. Tile: Jensen/Marineau Tile available through Country Floors

Pages 130 and 131. Photo courtesy Florida Tile Industries. Tile: Florida Tile

Page 133. Photo courtesy Epro, Inc. Tile: Epro

Page 135. Photos courtesy Pewabic Pottery. Tile: Pewabic Pottery. Photographer: Tim Thayer

Page 136. Photo courtesy Dennis Ruabon, Ltd. Tile: Dennis Ruabon

Page 137, item 118. Photo courtesy Latco Products. Tile: Latco Products

Page 137, item 119. Photo courtesy Starbuck Goldner Tile. Tile: Starbuck Goldner Tile

Page 138. Photo courtesy Dunis Studios. Tile: Dunis Studios. Photographer: Val Dunis

Page 139. Photo courtesy Architectural Accents. Tile: Architectural Accents. Photographer: David Marlow

Page 140. Photos courtesy Walker Zanger Tile. Tile: Walker Zanger. Designer: Nancy McCarthy. Photographer: Ed Goldstein

Page 141, item 124. Photo courtesy Diana and Tom Watson of Native Tile and Ceramics. Tile: Native Tile and Ceramics. Photographer: Alisa Wyatt

Page 141, item 125. Photo courtesy Alison Cooper. Tile: Alison Cooper Tile

Page 142. Photo courtesy Peter King and Marni Jaime. Tile: Peter King and Marni Jaime

Page 143. Photo courtesy Cheyne Walk, Inc. by permission Oehlschlaeger Gallery. Tile: Cheyne Walk

Pages 144 and 145. Photo courtesy Florida Tile Industries. Tile: Florida Tile. Photographer: Roger Miller Photo, Ltd.

Page 151. Drawing courtesy Mapei

Page 152. Drawings courtesy Mapei

Page 153. Drawings courtesy Mapei

Pages 156 and 157. Drawings courtesy Christine Mizak